A WOMAN WHO MADE
HERSELF HER MUSE

A WOMAN WHO MADE
HERSELF HER MUSE

a collection of poetry by

karissa strain

FORWARD

I write this as I have completed typing these poems into this manuscript. Going through each and every one was sort of a reckoning of me-a revisiting of an older version of myself. A version I know well but no longer resonate with.

I know I will continue to write about my life as a woman and experiences in my femininity and my journey to grow and expand and fully step into my womanhood, however, I know this manuscript is complete. I wrote these poems and passages at a time in my life where I was changing. A time when I was truly ready for change. The women I wanted to step into graciously found the woman I was being. She found her in a low place, she reached out her hand and plucked her from her shallows and walked with her onto the path she was meant to be.

You see, the me she found was a woman who was taking what she could get, a woman who let the men in her life dictate her worth, a woman who struggled to know what her voice stood for and a woman who did not yet know how to use her voice. The woman I am today has never been more sure of her voice. I stand on firm footing of my beliefs and passions and most importantly my purpose in this life.

This is the first time in my life I got very honest with myself. The thing I love most about art and being an artist is the vulnerability of it. The ability to cut your chest, rip it open and let your heart utterly pour from you. That's what this book is to me, coming to terms with all the hidden parts of me, the parts I no longer wanted to hide. There is strength and beauty in all that I am, in all that I've done. The moments of pride and the moments of hard lessons learned.

I spent years as a woman in the entertainment industry fighting with myself for not "being enough". My every move was dictated around waiting for the call to come, waiting to book the job, waiting to get the meeting that could change my life. I spent every moment worrying about how I was perceived, as if my value was determined by the number on the scale. What I ate, how I worked out, what I wore would divulge the woman I was. I spent so many years living to please the male gaze- always needing to remain my "most fuckable"- so I'd be hired, so I would catch the attention of the higher ups, so my ideas would seem more interesting and ultimately to convince the world that what I had was "sellable"…the reckoning I mentioned was the realization in my soul that I'd rather take it all to the grave with me then to sell my soul to the devil- an absolute injustice to all I have to offer. I continue to live my life by this to this day and will do so for every day forward. I only want what wants me equally. I have so much to offer through my passion and my pen that my physique could never come close to capturing.

I sprinkled a photo series of myself throughout this book as a reclaiming of ME- the me I know myself to be, the me that I wish to share with the world. Honest, natural, brave- with no intentions of posing to please anyone's eye but my own. A remembering, as I age, of the woman I am right now. Pleased with my body. Unashamed of my nudity and unafraid to expose every part of the woman I am. The woman who is proud of writing these words you are about to read, the woman who knows who she is and is unwilling to sway.

These photos are untouched originals straight from the photographer. A woman I met this year whom I hope to know better with time. Not just any woman, the first woman who reached out to me to tell me she saw something in me that inspired her. After years of working tirelessly in an industry where I was constantly grovelling, begging and borrowing for attention and representation, this woman came to me with hopes of representing me as a model. She came as an equal, not a superior. She came not asking me to change anything about myself, she came kind and considerate. She came, calling me art…and these photos are the art we made together. Two women trusting each other in safety and sisterhood in a world that loves to tear that essence apart.

Some of the images are stand alone and some are relayed as a series with the intention of capturing the movement of my body as opposed to showcasing a static image of a model with perfected posture. It was important to me to proudly portray the form and function of our bodies ability to "move" us through life as it expands and contracts- with purpose.

These photos show me, the real me- ALL of me. They show my bare body, the curves of my posture, the rolls of my skin, the imperfections. I didn't want to edit anything, I wanted to be seen exactly as I am. A burn mark on my arm from cooking dinner for my family. Red bumps near my breast because my cycle was upon me and my hormones made themselves present through my pores. Imperfect peaches of butt cheeks with a friction rash from the bike seat I teach spin classes to uplift and encourage woman through 3 times a week- still just as juicy and delicious ;)

I will not edit them- I am perfect exactly they way I am shown. May we all remember that! Thank you for taking this journey with me, I hope it helps guide you on your own. I hope you find a kin to your truth. I hope you find value in your vulnerability and I hope you have a knowing with your voice and are unafraid to use it.

May you find passion, may you find purpose, may you find YOU!

- Karissa

A Woman Who Made Herself Her Muse
Copyright © 2024 by Karissa Strain.

All rights reserved. This book or any portion thereof may not be reproduced or used in any manner whatsoever without the express written permission of the author except for the use of brief quotations in the context of reviews.

ISBN: 978-1-0689109-3-7

Photography by Tyg Davison.

Book design & layout by Rachel Clift.
rcliftpoetry.com

First printing edition, 2024.

@sistersstrain
sistersstrain.com
The Sisters Strain

special thanks

This book would not be complete without
the artistic eye and trustworthy talent
of Tyg Davison- Owner of Citizen Agency.

As a woman who is primarily a filmmaker and storyteller,
I am a huge fan of mixed media art.
I had a vision of self portrait photography to accompany
my written pieces and Tyg brought that dream to life.

It was so important to me to not showcase my body under the male gaze
with nudity as a means of inducing or soliciting desire from the viewer
but rather baring myself to honor and
appreciate the female form
for myself...
as all woman should
honor their own sensuality
and be proud of the forms of their femininity.

She provided a safe space to do exactly that,
and I am forever grateful.

poems

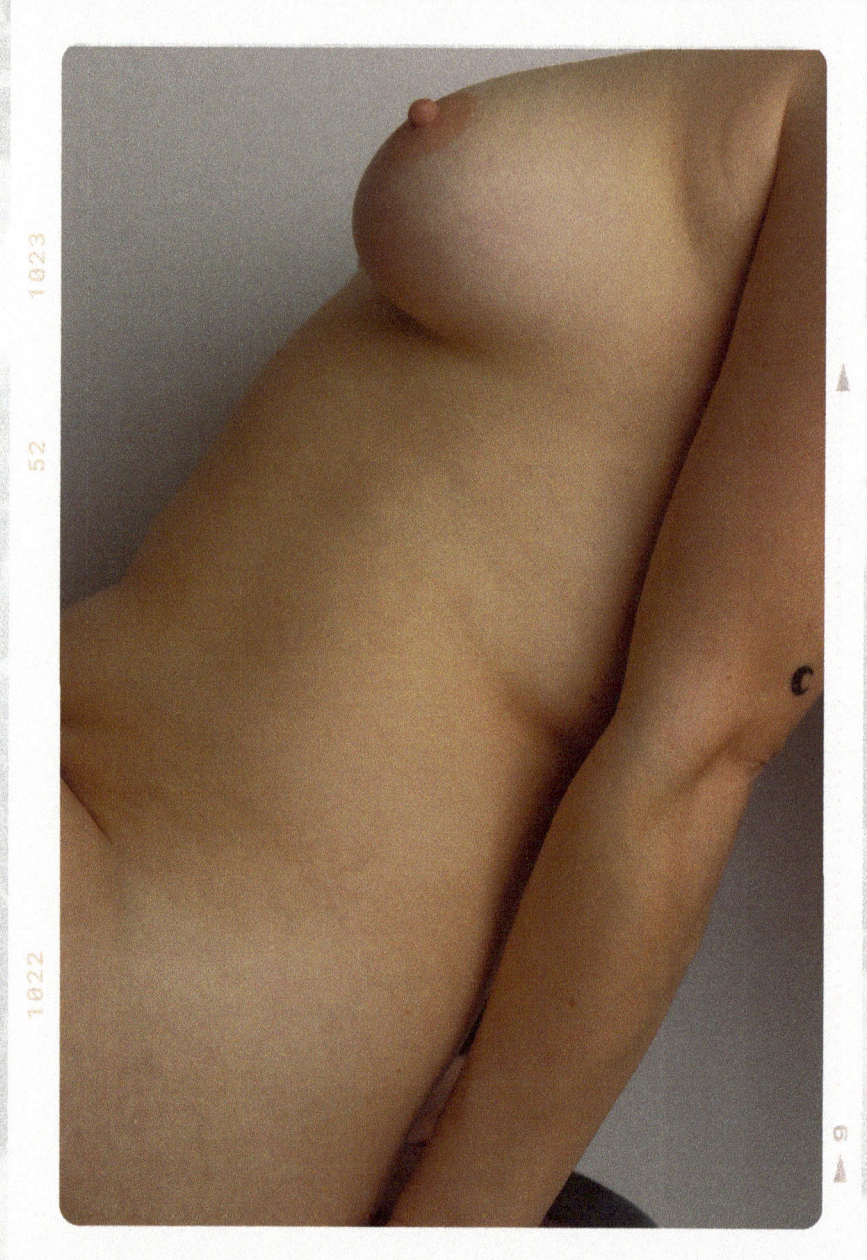

A WOMAN WHO MADE *HERSELF* HER MUSE

My head and my heart
are in two different places
I struggle to know which one is wrong

Both can't be right
and I need a little guidance
to tell me where it is I belong

One is my present
the other is my future
both hold firm ties to my past

But which one will win
and where will that take me
because this two-faced existence can't last

I grew up on the bank of a river
It was my hideaway because it's where I felt most found
It's been over 15 years since I felt it's muddy waters at my feet
but in my mind I go back there almost daily
I shared that bank with only my sister, few souls I've known
have ever heard it exists

It is so sacred to my very own existence

The trees deeply rooted that swayed overhead
and housed my secret treasures
are forever entwined in my soul
The fabric of me is knit of bark and leaves, mud pies,
waves lapping, fish jumping, the scent of pine
I had no idea what I wanted to be, but I knew who I was
Upon a stick that reminisced of a wishbone
I dreamt my dreams and set them free
Grandiose wishes for something bigger-
something better-
something great!

But what did that even mean to me then?
What does it mean now?

You see, I never asked
I just trusted it

It was some kind of magic that whipped through me
upon every soft breeze or brisk wind, every cubby in a tree stump
I found to hide a new treasure,
The squish of mud between my toes,
in every birds song,
every bugs crawl,
I understood it
and I felt it all

A WOMAN WHO MADE *HERSELF* HER MUSE

There is no other time, nor place in the world
that has held such understanding for me
We think as we get older and we learn and we grow
we become better versions of ourselves
We deny the little girl on the bank
and we write off her wishes

But today I woke up and I envy her
I admire her
I wish to dare to be more like her

What's so foolish about wishes-
even if you don't know what you're wishing for?
What's silly about grandiose plans-
who cares if they never come to fruition?
Where's the fault in dreaming-
even if those dreams never do come true?
And what's so trivial about sinking our toes in mud,
listening to the wind, feeling the thrill of a cool, wet wave
lap upon your bare skin
or finding treasures we keep secret to our soul?

If it has lasted in my memory for 15 years
it is clearly not so trivial to me
so why have I, for so long, denied that part of my being?

I'm still trying to figure that part out.

I dare me to do it.

I find my fear of complacency in constant combat
with my wonders of worth
I have big dreams, aspirational goals
I would never want to give up on
But they are still a ways off
from being realized
It feels like I have nothing but love and passion
to show for myself
Other than in the bank of the heart
these commodities hold no value

Still I wonder
How can a human bursting at the seams with so much life
feel like they measure so little

I scroll through images of starlets passed
Wondering if I fit the mould, if any images of their bodies
"allow" mine to exist.
As if they have the same thickness, the same curves,
that gives mine permission to take up space

Am I considered sexy still with broad shoulders and full arms?
Is my belly button tight enough to be considered fit but at the same time
are my hips wide enough to appear feminine?

We live in a time of fillers for lips and butts and breasts
but starve yourself to diminish the rest.
You can't jiggle or bounce, not even an ounce,
unless it's the exact right location
your fat chooses to flounce

I search and search and my fits hard to find
and I wonder what I have to give up to obtain or to buy it?

Is the outward appearance of my body indicative
of the success I could achieve as an artist?
Does one rely on the other?

Do I do things my way and strive to be the change
or do I succumb to the pressure and just play the game?

A WOMAN WHO MADE *HERSELF* HER MUSE

Trying to figure out how to bend the rules
while the defiant spirit raging inside of me duels.

I want to enjoy life and live it to the fullest,
don't want to give up the things that bring me joy,
that make me who I am
Don't want to strip myself of my natural womanhood.

Don't want to worry about the drinks or food I consume
as if they somehow defend the artistic presence that ensues

If I weigh less, will my comedic laughs weigh more?
If my waist is more cinched, will I be less of a bore?
If I plump a fake butt will acting bring me more luck?
If I show less cellulite will agents finally give a fuck?

What will it take for me to just accept
exactly who I am without needing to check
what anyone else does or did in the past

That's not my legacy

Not the mark I want to last

Why do we teach little girls to be so polite?

Polite little girls turn into women lacking will

Polite little girls put others before themselves,
to the detriment of their self fulfilling

Polite little girls do what they've been told
even when their hearts pull them in a different direction

Polite little girls live with a layer of guilt
encompassing all that they do

Polite little girls turn into women struggling
with the idea of being enough

But what is enough?

Who sets the standards?

Why do we give others the authority
to dictate what our enough is?

A WOMAN WHO MADE *HERSELF* HER MUSE

For so long I've apologized for being myself

I've placated and become more easily agreeable

I've catered my interactions specific to my audience

I've quieted my thoughts

I've minimized my mind

I've reworked my words

I've turned down my tone

I've gone along instead of going against

I've emoted less to appease egos more

I've bit my tongue, to not bite the hand that feeds

But what makes that hand more worthy than me?

A WOMAN WHO MADE *HERSELF* HER MUSE

Black as death
and dark as night
Slithered from a dream
straight into my psyche

An unwanted guest
of the most foul breadth
But I'm aware it is I
who invited it

I struggle, I crave
to release myself from it's reigns
Pull it clean from roots
infestingly rotted

Inked in my flesh
it shall forever remain
Mark of the curse
that yet holds me captive

The sensual serpent
that yields me no pleasure
Leaves me lonely
and feeling deserted

KARISSA STRAIN

My angst eats at me
A hunger I cannot palate

Some days I wake up
just wanting to be Godzilla

And stomp the whole fucking world

A WOMAN WHO MADE *HERSELF* HER MUSE

Spring whispers secrets she's been keeping close to heart
In blossoms she unburdens, drawn from the frozen ground
Maybe if she shares them, I'll rise wiser than the winter
She'll teach me all the ways I could be living more profound...

Like mountains of love live amongst luscious lakes of lavender and lilacs

Beauty is built into the breadth of each buttercups basin

Curiosities are as capricious as the come up of the crocus

Fortune's as fond of the fearless as he is the finding of the forsythia

Sensitivities although delicate can be as sinewy as sweet alyssum

Real relationships as un-rare as the reliable rhododendron

Hearty laughter intoxicates as highly as woodland creatures find the hyacinth

Perfection pales in comparison to the primrose and pansies pigmentation

Tenderness trumps travail at the touch of a tulips petal

And there's boldness and bravery in the burst of bleeding hearts

A WOMAN WHO MADE *HERSELF* HER MUSE

Sometimes I wonder if I'll ever be satisfied
If my hunger will ever be satiated
or if I'm destined to be a woman forever restless
Ever searching for more

Does more have no cap?
Do I aim to break through an impenetrable glass ceiling?

But if my hearts yearning and my paths destination
don't align-where did this feeling come from?
Why must I have it?

A bubbling constantly brewing beneath my bones
that leaves me no rest
It surges on the tide of my blood
With every pulsing pound of my life's beating drum

My anthem
My war cry
My siren symphony

In no way soothing, it settles me not

It rattles me
Charges me
Fires me up

Perhaps I'm the fool who believes in it so

I cannot
I will not
Won't ever let it go

What makes them cocky?
Is it in them from birth
Is it something they were told
then had to practise and rehearse

What makes them cocky?
Is it an anatomical right
Is it the part they have we're missing
that make ours a frightful plight

What makes them cocky?
Is it their voice with deeper tones
Does depth of sound make words more weighted
softer ours, mere background drones

What makes them cocky?
Is it when structures broadly tower
When bodies exert power
and cause more petite ones to cower

A WOMAN WHO MADE *HERSELF* HER MUSE

What makes them cocky?
Is it their rule with iron fist
How they convince of joint commitment
while adding side birds to their list

What makes them cocky?
Is it in their spreading seed
But our bodies are the incubators
and from our bosoms feed

What makes them cocky?
Makes them think the world they run
Is it fair of one to state
without our sex it can't be done

What makes them cocky
And makes us the pesterous bitch
The whole thing seems off balance
The systems flawed, unfair, it's glitched

I have many colors
I can paint upon my skin
I am a lover, I am a lion
Could be your foe or be your kin

There are few who know
My hidden tapestry within
Kept under lock and key
Until my trust, you do win

I don't take things too lightly
Or give of them too free
I've learned to take more time
False facades to inevitably see

If you won't strip your colors
Or disrobe your soul for me
Then all you'll ever know
Is what a chameleon I can be

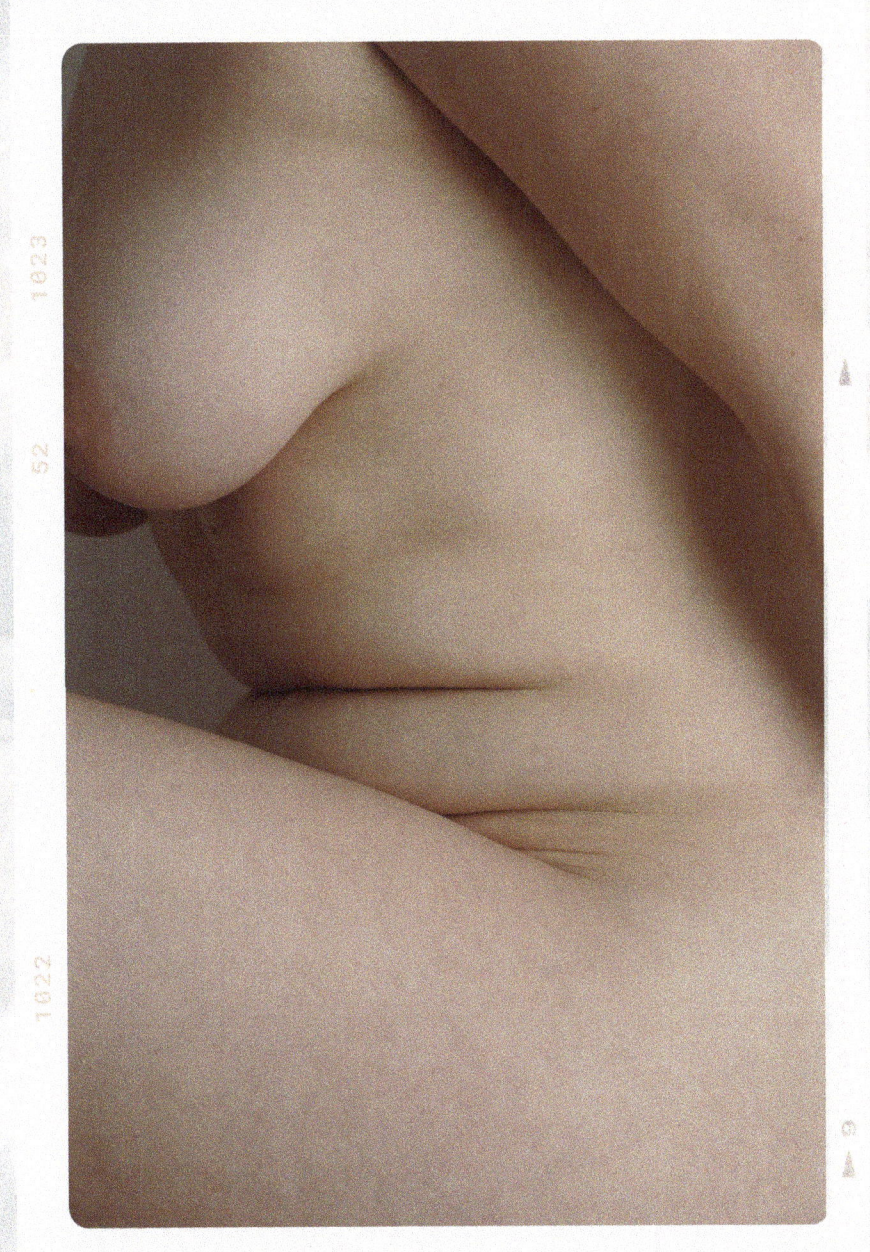

A WOMAN WHO MADE *HERSELF* HER MUSE

I had a dream I was a clown
dancing upon a giant pie
As other players came
and left the scene
more slices were taken
from the delicacy under my balance

As did the pie,
my footing grew increasingly scarce

I woke up wondering
how much of the pie remained
and how long I had
until I slipped
and was no longer dancing

I read somewhere "Love kills creativity"
For a brief moment I indulged the notion
It's been a long time since I've been wrapped up in the love of another
and here I am living the most creatively of my 30 years to date
Maybe there is truth to the sentiment
Maybe I must sacrifice a love life for the sake of my art

As if intimacy might tarnish my integrity
Of the mindset I must martyr for my muse
Somehow the void makes me more fruitful

I mulled it over a bit, but you know what?

I call bullshit
I call coward
I call fear

I recognize that fear as my own and know I am not above it
A few days pass without a poem and I wonder if I'll ever write one again

I want love
I want to find comfort in the arms of another
I yearn to know the feeling of home
And yet I'm terrified that contentedness will be my poetic undoing
The things I write about wanting will be the very things
that "take" writing from me

What if I lose my passion
My spark
My fire

A WOMAN WHO MADE *HERSELF* HER MUSE

What If I'm only ever pushed to the brink of expression
when my heart is lost or broken
What if sadness solidifies my stationary
Pining pushes my pen
Worthlessness weights my words
and without all of those wounds I wind up speechless?

But wait-
there it is again
Fear rearing it's ugly head

I say I am a woman who strives to never let fear stand in her way
or hold her back from fully embracing life
and yet here I sit
Stewing in a sea of my own insanity

Insane defined as doing the same thing
and expecting different results
So why then, do I fear change?

What makes me think staying in this state
will in any way bring me closer to the success I don't currently have?
Must the artist torture themselves for the sake of the art
or is that a choice in and of itself-choosing a torturous existence

I don't wish to be forever a tortured soul
I find the idea to be an utter waste of a life
And I find the notion ones art can only derive from low moments
to be a lazy attempt at being an artist all together

A WOMAN WHO MADE *HERSELF* HER MUSE

I've spent a lifetime of living
to fulfill others beautiful illusions
But finally YOU see the real me

Am I a beautiful doll with a 28" waist
With long flowing hair and plump lips to taste
If an hourglass shape I maintain
Full bosom, round buttocks
But a slender frame
Can dictate the beauty your eyes do behold
But not if I should stray
From the standard mould
A firm tongue lashing
A slap on the wrist
Chastised, criticized
My heart you do scold
Affronted, my unexpected emotions unfold
As the words cut deep
They leave a lasting impression
My soul, not my shape
Has learned a harsh lesson
I've done nothing wrong
By changing or growing
It's not about the figure of measurement
I'm showing

A WOMAN WHO MADE *HERSELF* HER MUSE

Shouldn't my value lie not
In the numbers on the scale
But my kindness, compassion,
How I chose love to heal
If my once doll-like beauty
Has faded in your eyes
Just because I have slightly plumper thighs
Than perhaps the word love,
Holds for us different meanings
Beauty to you, on the outside
I see in souls gleaming
I'm sorry I can't uphold
What you had hoped or expected

But it's been a long time coming now

That who I am I've accepted

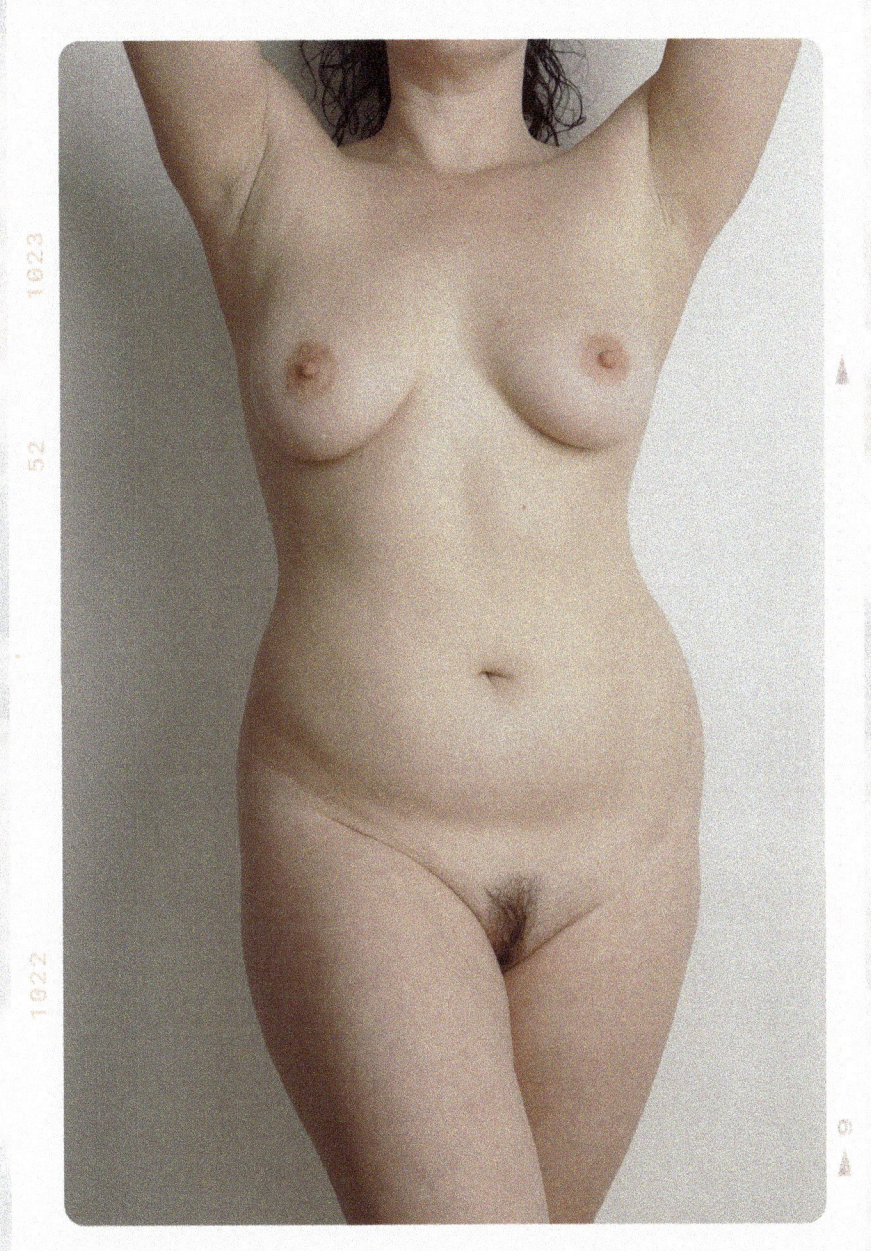

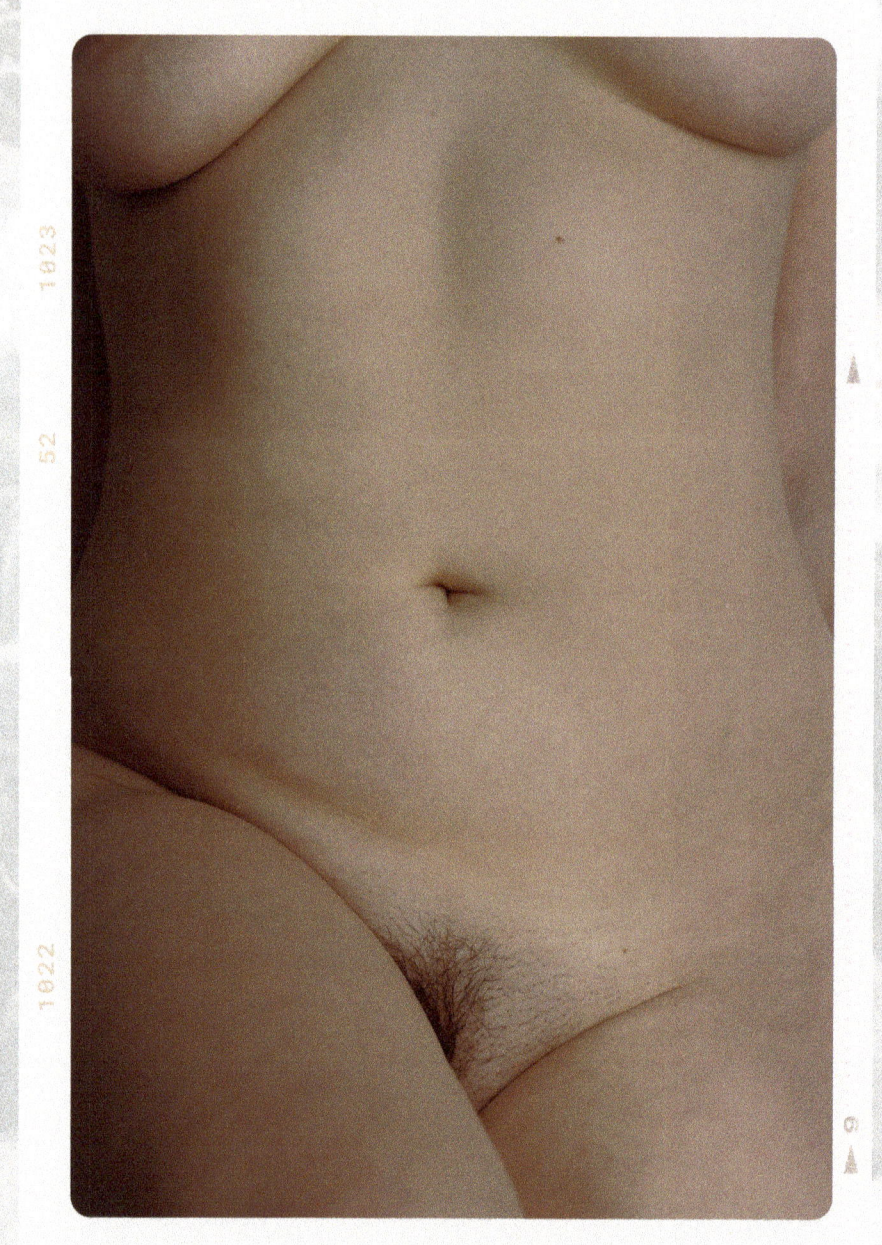

A WOMAN WHO MADE *HERSELF* HER MUSE

Resilience is a ruse that's been wreaking havoc
on my peace for years

Consider this my resignation.

From here forth I shall wear my weariness well
My fragility not feared to be futile
My vulnerability never again looked at as volatile

No longer shall I miss-take my misfortune,
for misfortune's been my maker,
my mystic muse

My ample adaptability will no longer to others adjust

My womanhood has been wriggled and writhed
in so many ways

My worries made out to be mere weeds-
swiftly plucked from an unsightly garden
Knowing full well it is not the last time they rear their ugly heads
For each one plucked leaves three more in it's wistful wake

This time my figure refuses to bounce back to its former shape
Bearing no ill so as not to burden others

I cannot swallow the seeds of another burden
as if it's existence was never germinated in my mind
While over time the roots fully tether
and blossoming branches threaten to break through my bones
Exposing the lush foliage of my leering layers
laden in my skin

I won't wear a sweet disposition upon smiling lips
while inside my sensitive soul shakes

Unable to house the trees fully forming inside me

Too full for my frame

A WOMAN WHO MADE *HERSELF* HER MUSE

Seeds are meant to be planted and tended to
in environments apt to expand with them

The potential of my personage as their potting
has been too long overwhelmed

Each seed shall be respectfully rooted and replanted
in a garden of which I'll tend

My head, not my heart
shall feel responsible to house them

Knowing the deepest roots lead to the woods high rise
Nutrient soil is necessary for new growth
and the buds must be honored
just as highly as the blossoms

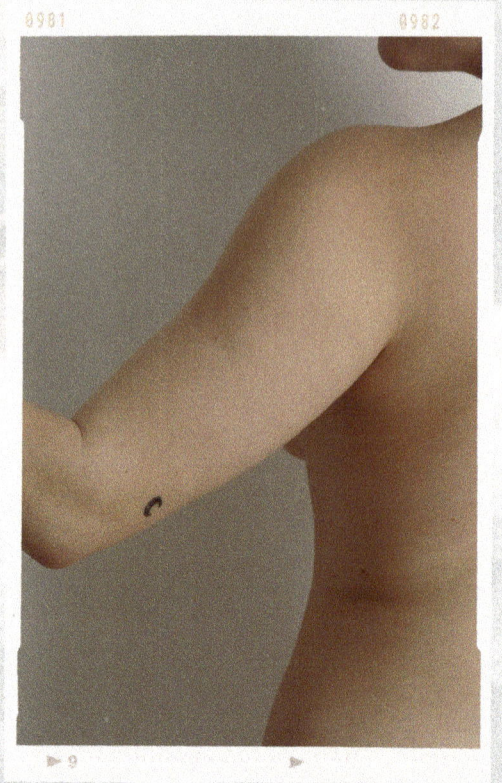
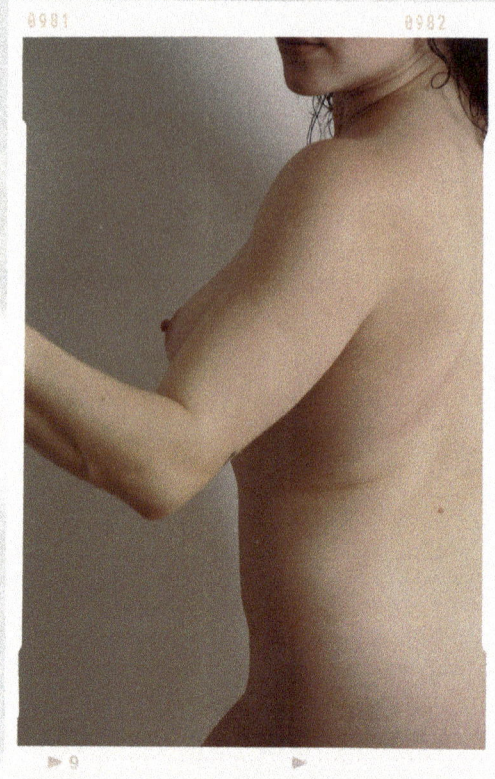

A WOMAN WHO MADE *HERSELF* HER MUSE

We are all simultaneously the branches
on someone else's tree as well
as the roots of our own

There are men aged mature
who've already lived it through

They'll get stars in their eyes
upon the meeting of younger you

They thought they had forever
and only wanted the single life

Then Mid-life finally hits them
and they panic for a wife

They want a second chance
to do the things they've never done

There's no turning back the clock
to avoid the setting of the sun

Sands long passed through their hourglass
they try to replenish with your own

Pluck you straight out of your world
set you a stage inside their home

You'll pay to play the part
young doting mother and hot wife

Give up any plans you had
to live as co-star to his life

A WOMAN WHO MADE *HERSELF* HER MUSE

They'll never understand
why you would ever choose to pass

You've got the looks and fertile body
they've got the status and the class

It's no match made of love
time not spent to know the real you

More an idea in their mind
based on appearance, you'll be held to

I guess it works for some
eager to accept and fill the role

But I know in my honest heart
it'd wear far too heavy a toll

I still feel rather young
with so much living left undone

I'd never give or trade my youth
as second wind to anyone

Venerated in Venus.

Admired in Aphrodite.

Idolized in Isis.

Adored in Astarte.

MELIORA IN ME

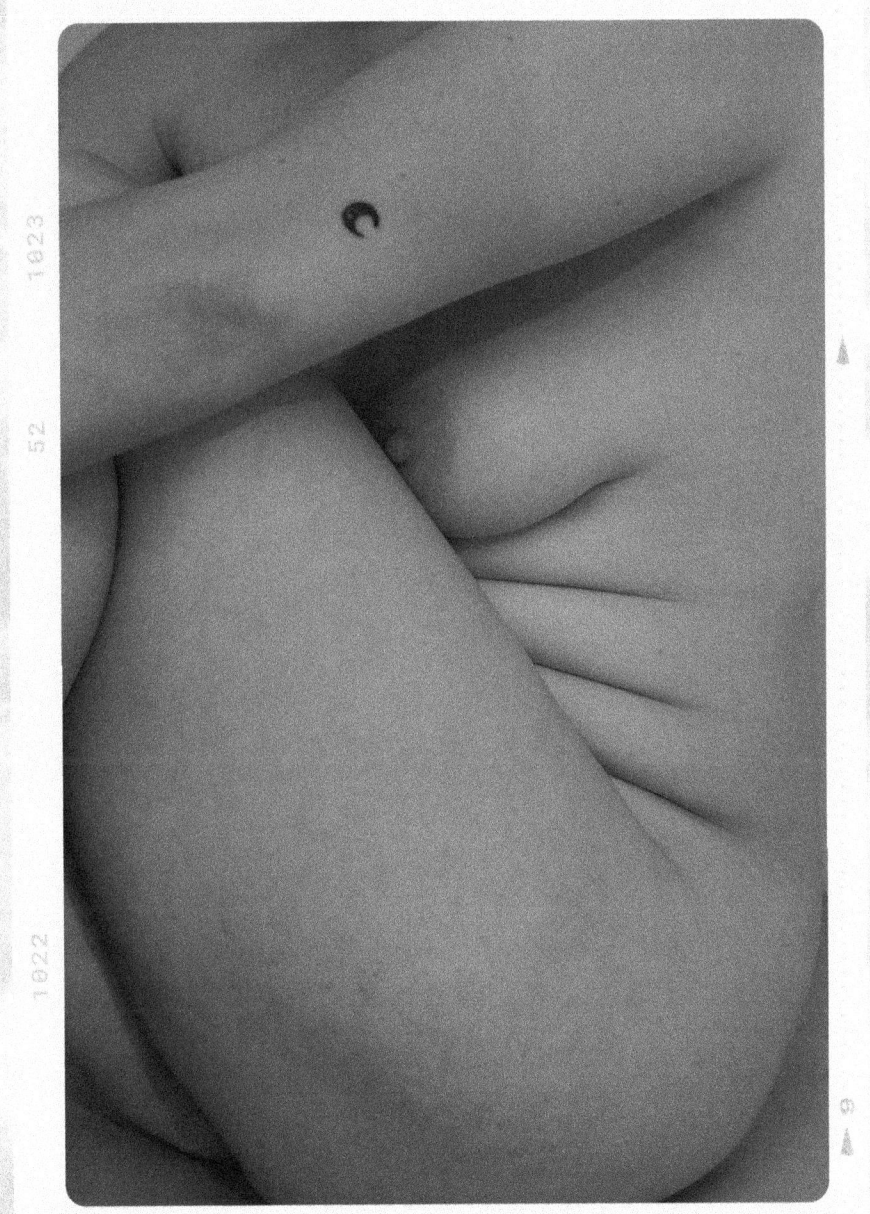

You're damned if you do
You're damned if you don't
You can play the whore
or you can play the hound

Vainly born to our beings
Domineering as genetics
To our male counterparts
loyally bound

If it pleases their eye
It pleases our reflection
Satiate their palate
they'll grant you your crown

The only true testament
To judge whether worthy
Is to strip you of your
adorned gown

A WOMAN WHO MADE *HERSELF* HER MUSE

There were things in my past I wanted no part of
so I toughened up and pushed straight through them
Recently I've noticed them rear their ugly heads
as insecurities pertaining to my past

I don't want to feel the weight of old wounds
or let their attachments keep me tethered
It's time to go back, to make myself feel it
rip the scars apart moment by moment

Process the baggage I couldn't carry then
not tip toe around but learn how to get past it
I'll never be free, won't truly be me
if I deny their dark shadow of existence

I cut myself, ready to cleanse myself
free my bloodlines of their poison
I'll dive a little as I delve, to release myself
of the shackles, guiltless of such burdens

KARISSA STRAIN

I wait on no one
with baited breathe
No photo liked
No comment left
No one's response
to leave me forlorn
No questioned intentions
creating feelings torn
No one to make
or to break my day
No one else has the power
to make me feel a certain way
No one to fit in
No schedule to please
Never again reduced
to begging on my knees

A WOMAN WHO MADE *HERSELF* HER MUSE

I will post for no one
if not for myself
My affections, for now
will be put on the shelf
Unlike the past
I won't be so quick to trust
Craving the real thing
not mere moments of lust
My intentions are clear
should our paths ever cross
Not one to confuse
or leave others at a loss
It's not that I've changed
I'll always be a lover
But I need to love myself
before giving to another

A WOMAN WHO MADE *HERSELF* HER MUSE

I've always been drawn to surrounding myself
in elements of nature that are much more
grandiose than myself

Skyline stretching oceans with their
depth and dicey waves

Endless views of rolling fields
kissing bright blue skies

Midnights brilliant blanket
of starry constellations

The tallest rows of buxom
branched trees

They've never made me feel small
in comparison
They've always made me feel hopeful-
Like I have room to grow

All these years I thought I was truly living for myself
But recently it has dawned on me
That there has always been another presence at the front of my story
I am a lover and I like that about myself
but why have I had this notion
that putting love for myself first was selfish?

Is it a universal thing, is it an inherently female thing?
Is it something you must learn through your adolescence
and perhaps I was just late to the realization?

Or maybe it has to do with humble beginnings
Growing up in a salt of the Earth, hard working,
not very well-off family

I was taught to do the right thing and follow the rules
and to never ask for too much-and maybe that's it right there
not wanting to ask for too much

I want love
I NEED love
But why have I thought that love must come
from another person
when I am, in fact, the biggest lover I know?

Why do I give of it freely to others
and yet ration the amount I'm willing
to express to myself?

Why has it taken me 30 years to give myself permission
to love me more...

A WOMAN WHO MADE *HERSELF* HER MUSE

She's all warrior but she's grown weary
She's all winner but she has not yet won
She's all heart but she feels half loved
She's all soul but she sees only superficial
She's all friend but she is foiled by foe
She's all dreams, disappointed by what she has to show

She's all team but she's left on her own
She's all soft but she is met with callous
She's all brains but she is beat out by brawn
She's all strength but told she's too sentimental
She's all sweet but she is ravaged by storm
She's all truth but her belief in integrity is torn

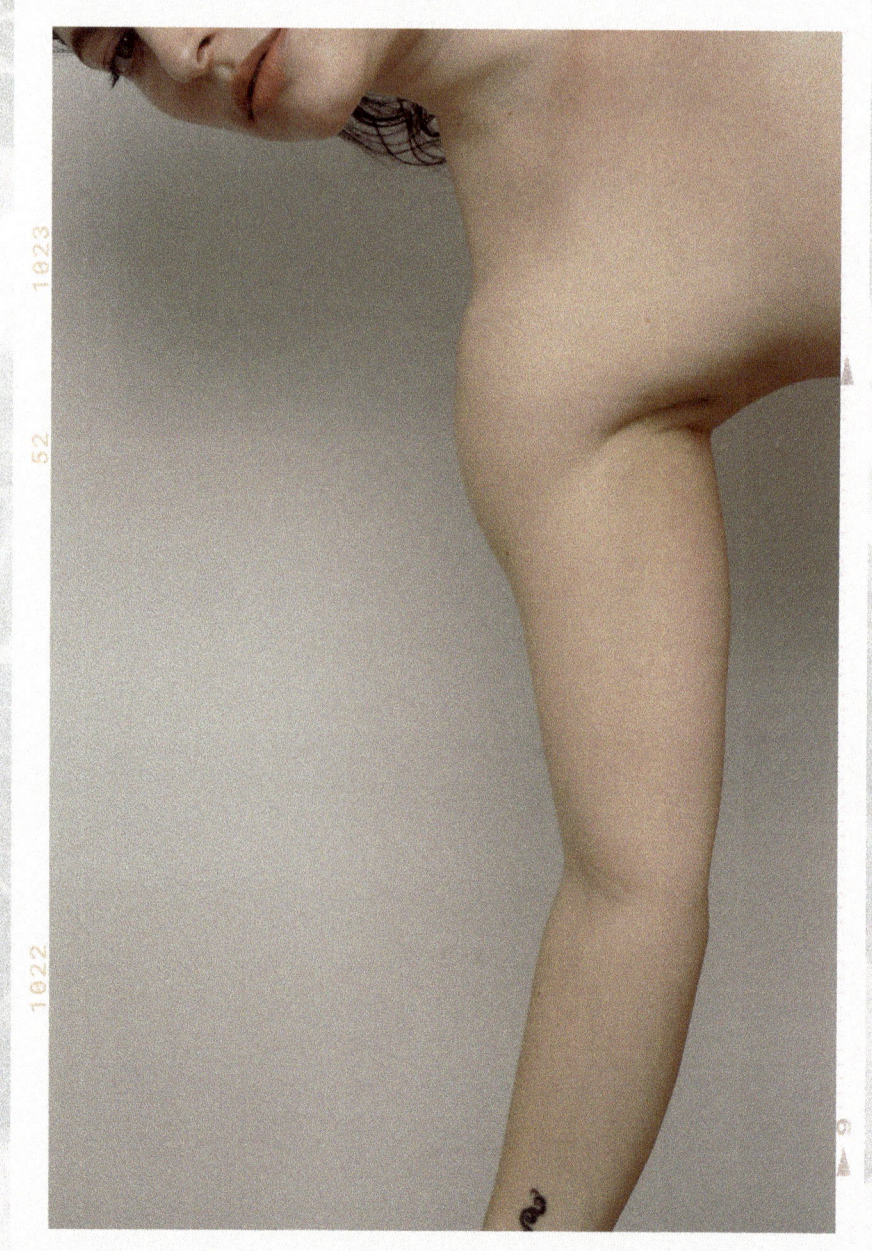

A WOMAN WHO MADE *HERSELF* HER MUSE

I consider myself a lucky one
Though I'm not monetarily blessed
My assets hold no value
Above that which I carry in my chest
So often underestimated
It fuels my defiant will
What I lack in my bank account
I more than exceed in my heart's thrills

You'll always be a moon in my sky
Too far away to touch up close
But you've kept my dark nights lit for so long
My most beautiful and precious ghost

It seems heaven certainly helped
This fool who thought she fell in love
In a sombre time of darkened doors
You were the pure and peaceful white dove

A gift that was undeserved
Of such fickle and fragile confines
We were a story never to be written
A love left to live between the lines

The sad woman of my solemn past
For my fierce future self once pined
Had I been wiser, stronger, braver
Maybe then I could have made you mine

They say the best things always disappear
And I knew I couldn't keep you here
But I often wonder what you would have become
If I could have kept you near

My sweet Ophelia, you fulfill your name
You've helped me in ways you'll never know
I hardly met you, but I see you in my dreams
It's through you, my love continues to grow

A WOMAN WHO MADE *HERSELF* HER MUSE

This is not the first time in my life I have felt my spirit die
My soul depleted
In fact, I've become accustomed to living
through such deaths

No matter how often I find myself stuck in this gutter
Drowning in the rain water as it rushes to the sewers
on the spiteful spirit of the storm
I still want to be lost in it

To give myself fully over to it
To be engulfed in it and it alone
A selfish hungry desire

But I constantly must share of it
With tasks undeserved of my attention
Tasks that harden my heart
Tasks that misinterpret my mind
Tasks not intended to take up my lifetime

When does the rain cease?
When will the winds whirl no more?
When will I reap the rewards of my investments?

Failure no longer foils me
So little off which I live
Yet the depths of my well of being
holds so much more to give

She's the arrows edge
The sharpened point that guides me straight
My trusted compass showing true North
When I'm lost, lonely, irate
When my heart is feeling restless
She calmly lets me roam
My skies bright and shining star
She always leads me home
She burns fierce in the darkness
She shades me in the light
She can talk me off the ledge
She can spark my inner fight
She'll lash me with her tongue
When she feels I'm out of line
She sits patient in the silence
Searching, eager for a sign
She's a lover, she's a lion
She protects whom she adores
She is kindness and compassion
Even to those she abhors
Her flames are all consuming
Her water's dark and deep
When faced with any challenge
There's no height she wouldn't leap
She is truth, she is intention
She is honest through and through
She is my sister, she is my soulmate
She is love that's always true

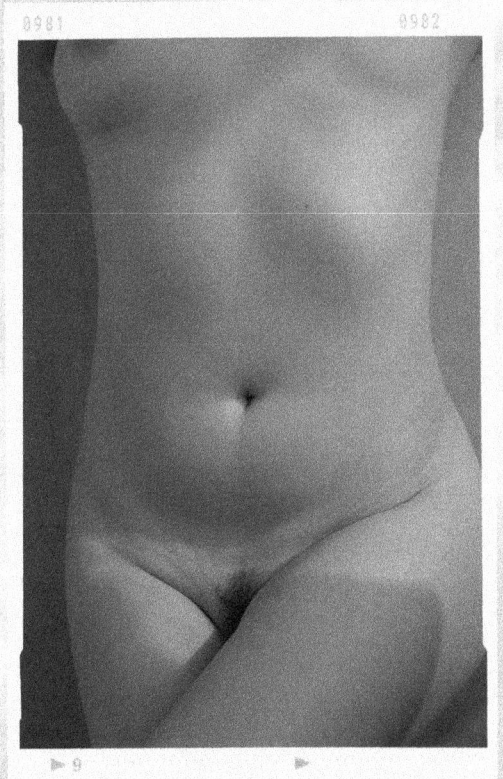
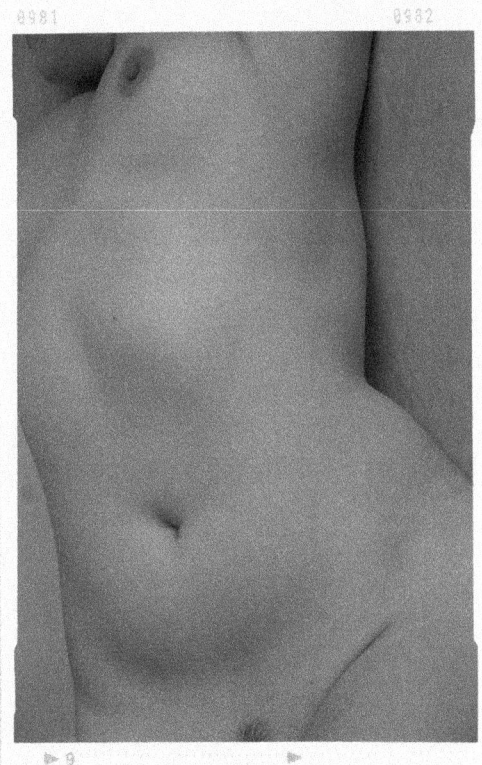
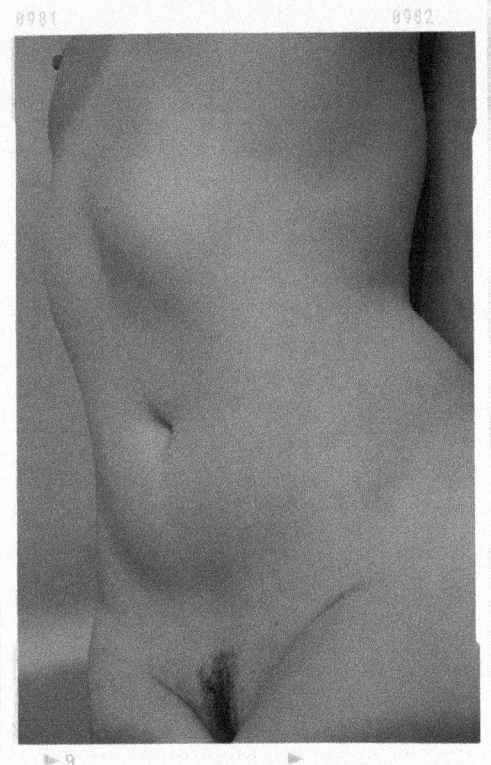
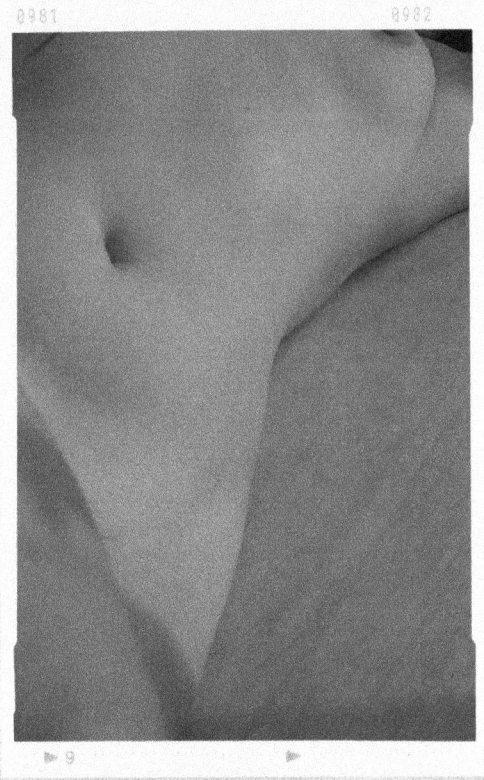

What is destiny but a dreamer's desire?
A longing, a calling
Living, breathing, reaching higher
An unimagined landscape on a canvas untouched by brush
A body calling to a beat in a dance unchoreographed
Words unwritten, all their power held back by the pen
Prose without purpose threatens never to be read
Instruments untuned, to the ear compose sore sound
A story still unfolding, plot lines begging to be bound

Lovers hands, lovers lips, lovers kept from warm embrace
Soul mates undiscovered, romance gone without a trace

What is love with no romance
Sleep without dreams
A life with no purpose
Empty existence it would seem

Is it wrong to dare
To believe a paths in place
Without a fateful destiny
Life seems unfruitful to face

A WOMAN WHO MADE *HERSELF* HER MUSE

Felt so close to you the first night
I kept craving our connection
The words came less
Attention faded
Left me longing for your affections

Lost in fantasies of what could be
Against what's tangibly in front of me
Can't place hope
In possibilities
Sleeping or waking, dreams I must flee

Reality dawned as harsh as it does
Nothing to be done to close this distance
Nothing more
Than misplaced passion
Caught in gratification of a kismet instance

Stars crossed these lovers paths
For the second pausing plight
Time it seems
Not on our side
Just two ships passing in the night

A WOMAN WHO MADE *HERSELF* HER MUSE

The moon cycles through
and as too do we
Mother natures presence
inherent to our destiny

A god given process
our born sex doth choose
Yet when it is upon us
our holiness we lose

The moon is made a marvel
admired from afar
But the beauty of our bodies
is not seen as on par

We watch as each month goes by
while it both wax then wanes
We commend it for it's effortless
adaptability to change

But what we make of women
their remarkability viewed in vain
Such cycles stand as a curse
as men's enduring bane

This sentimental heart hurts at the simplest of things
A note
A look
A word
and it comes unhinged

I wonder why the feelings affect me so

Are they due to my reading too much into things
Is it self sabotage setting in
Is it just minor aches from the bruises of my softness
or does my heart know something I do not

I heed it's warnings
though I hear not an explanation
And I wonder if it's safer for me to protect myself with it's cautions
or if staying in the confines of that safety
is what will end up hurting my heart the most

A WOMAN WHO MADE *HERSELF* HER MUSE

Here I sit in a stream of tears
My blood burns hotter than the furnace
My hearts been broken a thousand times
For a love I cannot touch or taste or see or most times even hear
Yet it's intangibility sways me not
This foolish heart's kept yearning
Faithful defendant till death
I care nothing of it's innocence

I'm not a praying woman
But this love brings me to my knees
I do not beg, but I borrow of it's fickle affections
Prayers unanswered couldn't stop
The moving pictures of daydreams
I wade through in the whimsical world of my mind
Wishing so badly to be lost in them
So that I may finally be found

Lovesick I never surrender
Though the weight of it wears me down
Pulled in a million directions
But my true north always known
I crave the freedom to strip my figure of distractions
Nakedly follow that star till it leads me home

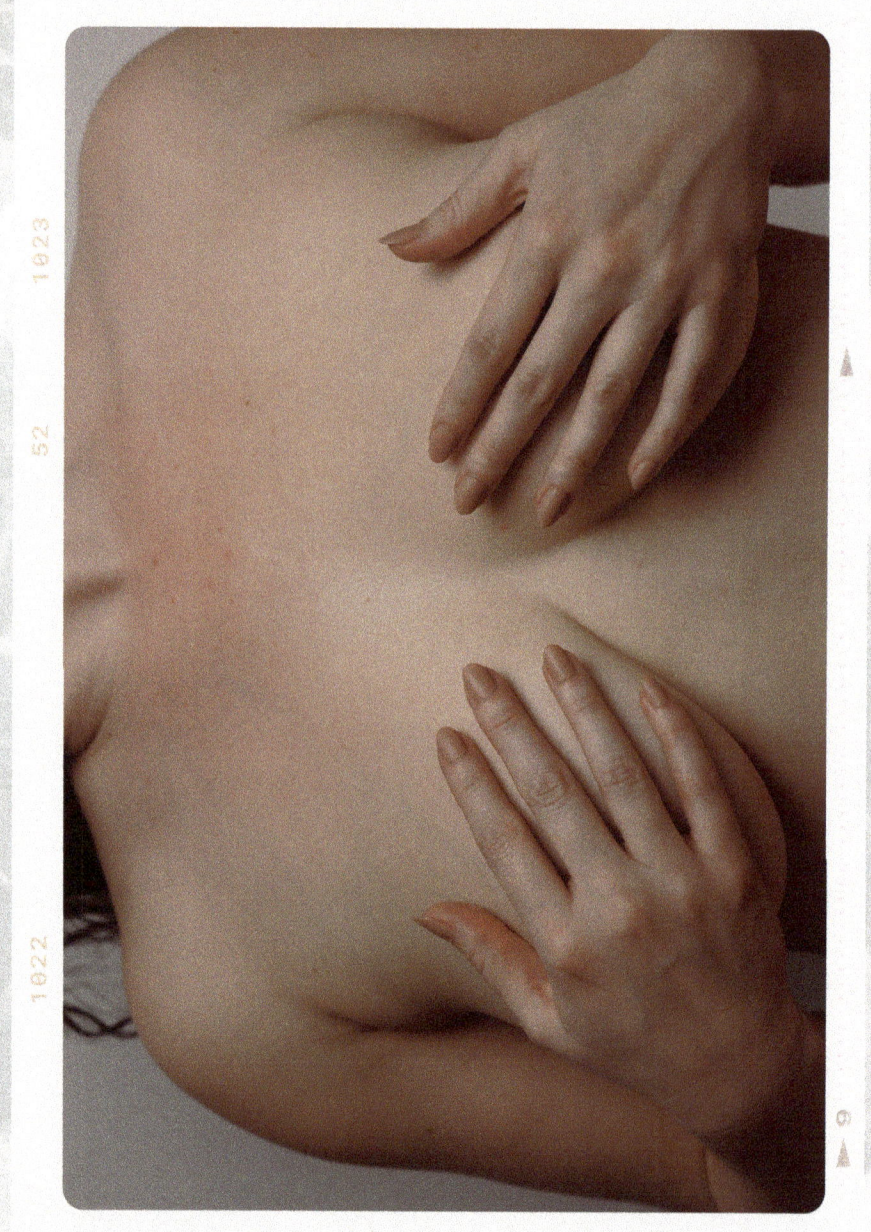

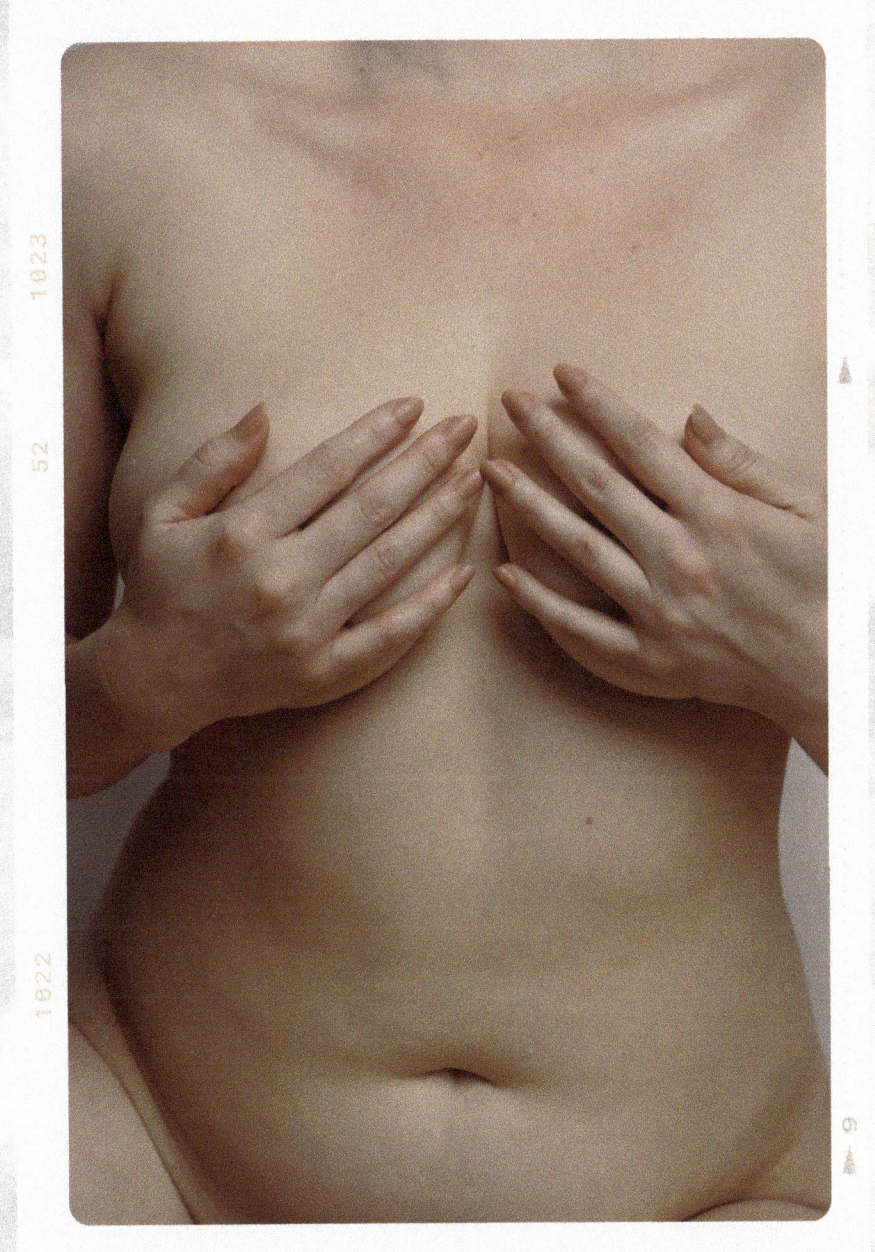

A WOMAN WHO MADE *HERSELF* HER MUSE

I must bat away the jealousy
and see you as you are
A woman deeply empowered
I admire from afar
I don't want to be you
but like you, to myself be true
Respect the different paths
our lives have travelled through
I see you as a wildling
Natural, bold and brave
No make-up, flowing hair
never to be a mans slave
Your words are deeply moving
Political, poignant and proud
In the presence of the masses
you'll always stand out in the crowd
Every time I see you
A fear creeps up in me
Not because you scare me
You liberate the woman I can be
For so long we've stayed quiet
Polite with pleasantries
Your presence brings an echo
My inner voice longing to be free
I commend you for your courage
Applaud your audacity
You've helped wake me from the woman
to the wolf it's time to feed

You test me
You taunt me
You toil with my temper
Your kisses and your hugs
the most invaluable of treasures
You've shown me the roots
of the word unconditional
Even when my patience passes
your presence has been pivotal
Your laughter is the sweetest
sound that I've heard sung
You embrace me with a warmth
that burns brighter than the sun
Your mischief knows no bounds
At times you are a terror
But the lengths I would go for you
will never know a barrier
Your energy's explosive
as the beating of my heart
Your blood is mine
Our souls entwined
You will always be a part

~of me~

A WOMAN WHO MADE *HERSELF* HER MUSE

I have failed
and what a glorious thing that is
For it no longer holds
the capacity to shock me
Now I can begin
to allow myself success

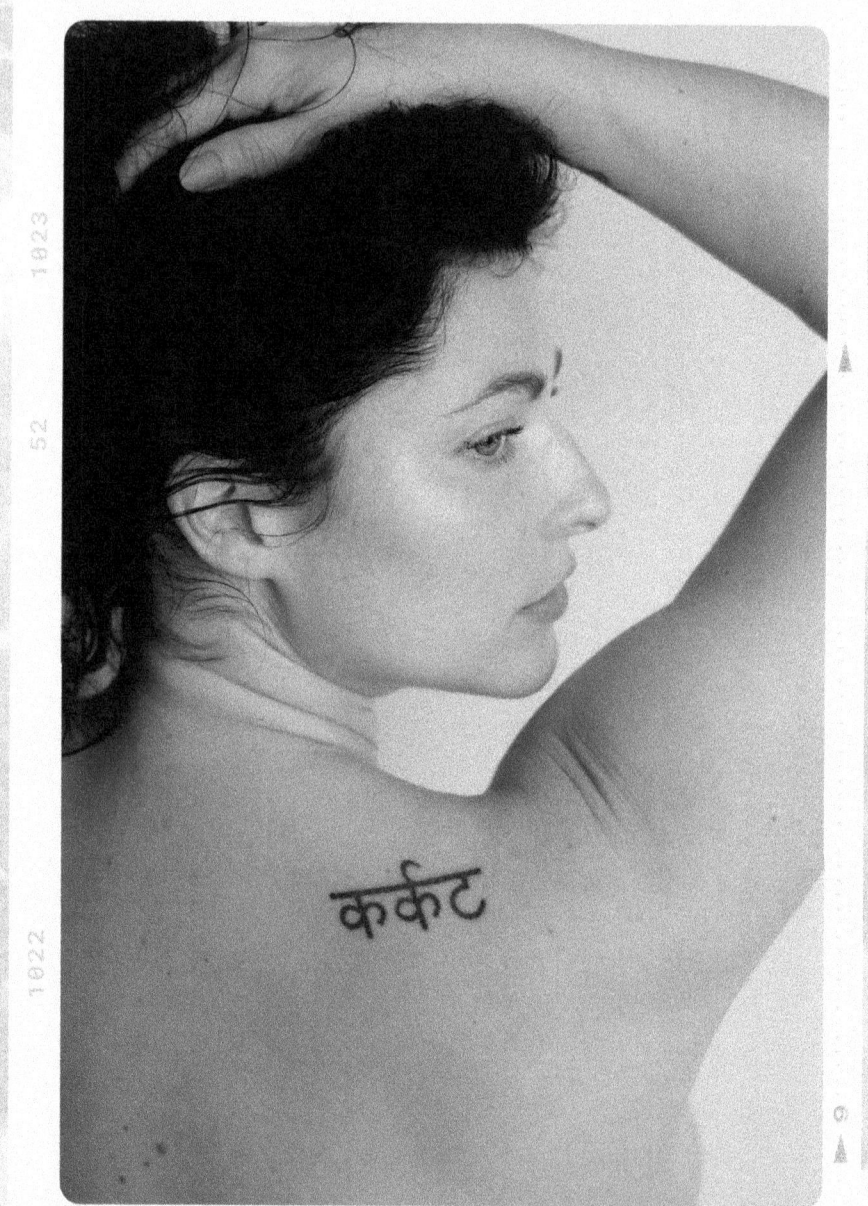

A WOMAN WHO MADE *HERSELF* HER MUSE

I think entirely too much about being grounded
that I weigh my own dreams down

My grounding drowns my dreams

She never thought she was beautiful…

She carried the weight of the world
upon her soft, slender shoulders
A soldier with no training, sheathed sword or shield
The older of 7 she fit her role rightfully,
responsibilities graciously accepted

Only a child herself
she grew up too fast
filling shoes with space for at least 3 more sizes
Who was she? She had yet to learn
No time for fumbling or finding her footing
No matter the terrain she marched right through
A vulnerable army relying on her guidance
Parents gone too soon she became one herself,
her own offspring as well as her siblings

No longer the daughter, the sister or the lover-
A matriarch to her lineage whether ready or warranted
Never the beauty queen nor belle of the ball
A debutante coming out more young warrior
than young woman

A WOMAN WHO MADE *HERSELF* HER MUSE

Her prowess poured into each person
who's path she paved
Every ounce of her shared, none kept to herself
A ladder to step up
A bridge to cross
A hand held to whoever's in reach

I wouldn't be me if she hadn't been she-
her soul sacrifice gave me full hearted freedom

She is my mother
A warrior woman to be reckoned with
The belle of my ball
An unwavering vision

KARISSA STRAIN

All I've got is this island
Let go of the rest
Straddling the sea of unknowns

Stripped my soul naked
Hold ties to no place
Intuition my compassionate compass

Wonders of worth
Seep through the seems
I patch and pretend don't exist

Heat comes and goes
Such untimely dismissal
Little drummer boy rattles my nerves

Meant as a temporary
Yet humbly remains
My one and only constant

Lavished in satin
Lights twinkle above
The most mountain to make

~of this molehill~

I dream so big I despise myself for it
If I wasn't held down by flesh and bones
I might float away with my mind
A moonstruck butterfly

I ride the roller coaster higher as I keep building bigger,
Heart pounds harder,
Love let lust hungry

Wavelengths set no limits,
Passions no holds barred

And it comes
And it comes
And it COMES

Crashing into me

Crashing out of me

A WOMAN WHO MADE *HERSELF* HER MUSE

Words on blank page
Image struck to canvas
Whatever I want, it IS

Until my sentimentality is sobered
The curse of creativity
For fortune's sold me fables

The ride comes to an end

Abrupt
Breathtaking
Over as quick as it began

...until I dare dream again

This 5 am silence
seems unnervingly loud
It keeps me from falling
to slumber

Wondering what reason
I remain awake
Why dreams have failed
to take me under

My mind has won
the moment eyes wake
Thoughts barely held back
like the dawn

The air is crisp
Clenched blankets, I shiver
Bones feel damp
as the dew upon the lawn

Do you ever feel a pull so strong
in the deep depths of your heart?
I feel it
It radiates through my body
It gives me hope and makes me hungry
It shakes my core
making me feel sick
I feel a surge of love and I feel abandoned
Passion runs through my veins
hot as molten lava
building up to the explosion

I know it means something
I know I'm supposed to do something
It's my body dilating
Contractions unbearable
Ready to give birth…but to what?

Is it a poem, a song
Or is it just quiet begging to be sought
Is it nature chastising me
for neglect of recognition
Is it wanderlust?

I need to move
I need to go
I need to think
I need to cry
I need to FEEL
I need something-

ANYTHING

A WOMAN WHO MADE *HERSELF* HER MUSE

Inspire me

Pour from me

I'll use a pen
I'll use my words
I'll use my body
I'll use anything to make it stop

How can I feel so much I feel nothing?

How can I feel so full I feel empty?

How can I feel so upheaved I feel comforted?

My heart fucking hurts
It aches
It throbs
It constantly taunts me
An insatiable palate-it's a picky eater
I don't know what to feed it...

But it's refusal to swallow
leaves my whole body starved
I'm left to bare bones
My dehydrated mouth parched
Rendered speechless

I want to be sweet again
I want to be sweet and not fear it
will take away my strength

I fell in love with him
I trusted him
He told me he loved me
I trusted him
He took my virginity
I trusted him
He told me to go off birth control for my hormonal health
I trusted him
He told me he would pull out
I trusted him
He said whatever choice I made he would be there
I trusted him
He spent time with someone else while I was carrying
I trusted him
He said he could never love a woman who birthed a child
because he wouldn't be attracted to them after giving birth
I trusted him
Too embarrassed to tell anyone but him
I trusted him
He didn't come to the appointment
I trusted him
He left me alone to deal with it
I trusted him
I suffered in silence
I trusted him

A WOMAN WHO MADE *HERSELF* HER MUSE

Why did I trust him over myself?
As if his 6 years my senior
gave him seniority

The relationship ended
along with the conception

He gets to walk away
unweighted by bodily effects

I will carry it all my life

You said we've known each other for many years
as a suitable reason for me to pick up and come to you
An enticing photo posted the only reason you recall me
after silence stretching seasons

The truth is you never really did know me
I was always more libations liberal madness
than I was myself
You loved to toil in my troubles
and then torment me with your turbulence
When I cried for help you just called me crazy
Your affections were as fickle
as the footing we were both standing on
They teach schoolyard kids
two wrongs don't a right make
But I think we both missed that lesson
because I always felt your matching of my wrongs
could make the two of us together
more mercifully right

I am a hopeless romantic, a dreamer
I believe in love and happiness
I believe in humanity
I will always give someone the benefit of the doubt
I believe people can change
I will give them a second, a third
countless chances to prove themselves

This mindset undoubtedly leads to a lot of heart ache and disappointment
and I am discouraged from it constantly
but no matter how hard I try, how many times I get hurt
I will never give up, I can't
it's simply not in my nature

I'll always give people the chance
to prove my hope in them right
Some may view this as foolish or naïve
but I don't think that

I think we've grown accustomed to giving up
and writing off too easily
Just because you do something shitty
that doesn't make you a shitty person
We all have our story and our reasons that drive us

I hold out for that instance when something great
and unexpected happens
When someone otherwise "doubted" comes through
All they needed was someone to believe in them
and someone to let them know they can be better
That they never have to be perfect
The love and belief in them will not falter
even if they mess up or fail

A WOMAN WHO MADE *HERSELF* HER MUSE

We must remember that every rose has it's thorn
to every life there comes an eventual death
and for every day the night too must fall

Life's not always perfect and clean cut and easy
It's not always as simple as black and white
and it definitely doesn't always make sense

But the world is full of beauty and opportunity
as long as you're looking at it through
open and gracious eyes

So dare to dream
always believe
and never be afraid to take chances
even at the cost of heartache

Broken hearts can always be mended
but regrets are never easy to swallow.

KARISSA STRAIN

I am but love
in the caress of a woman
I know no other way to be

My heart set ablaze
My mind a wild fire
Crave the cool tides of your sea

I long to embrace
the feeling of you
For you to fully feel me

Enrapture my soul
Envelope my skin
Lover, set my hunger free

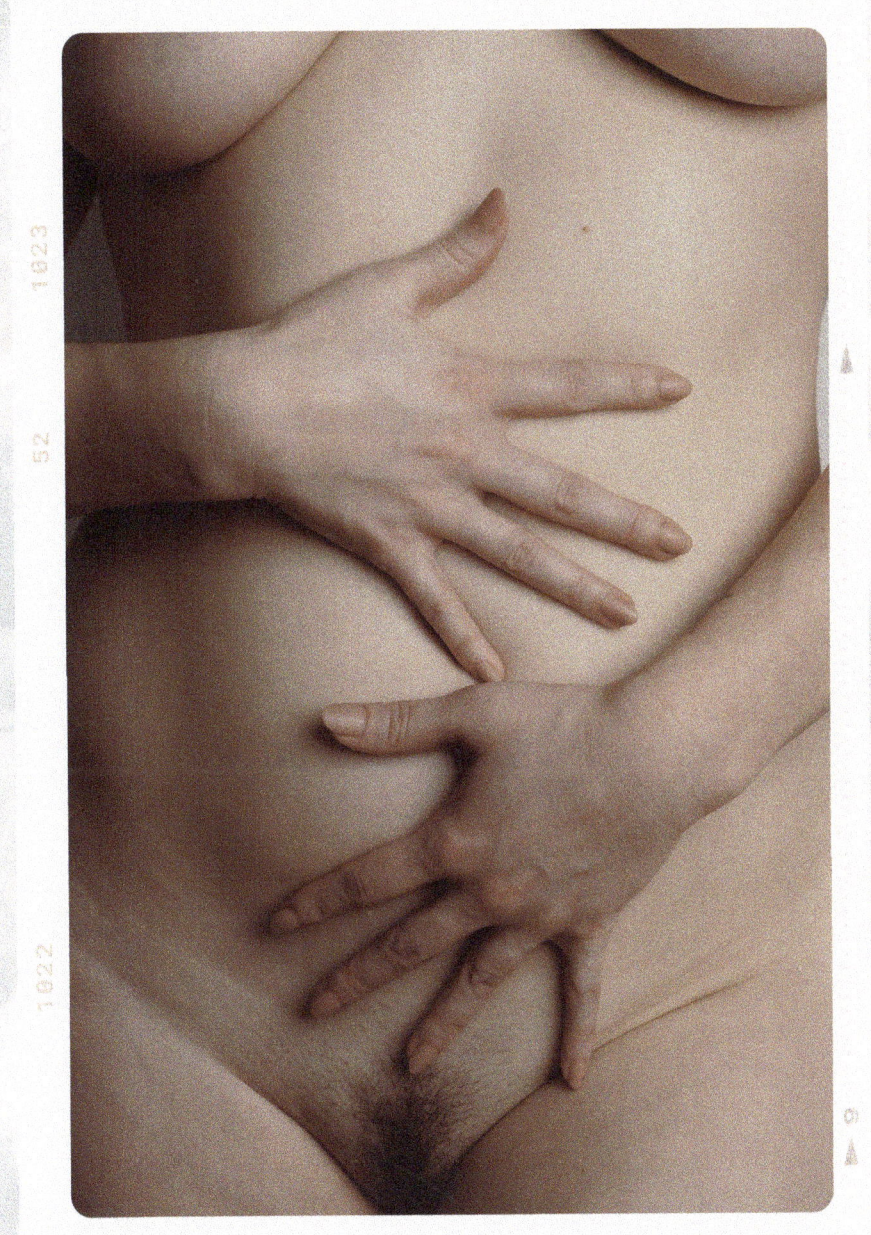

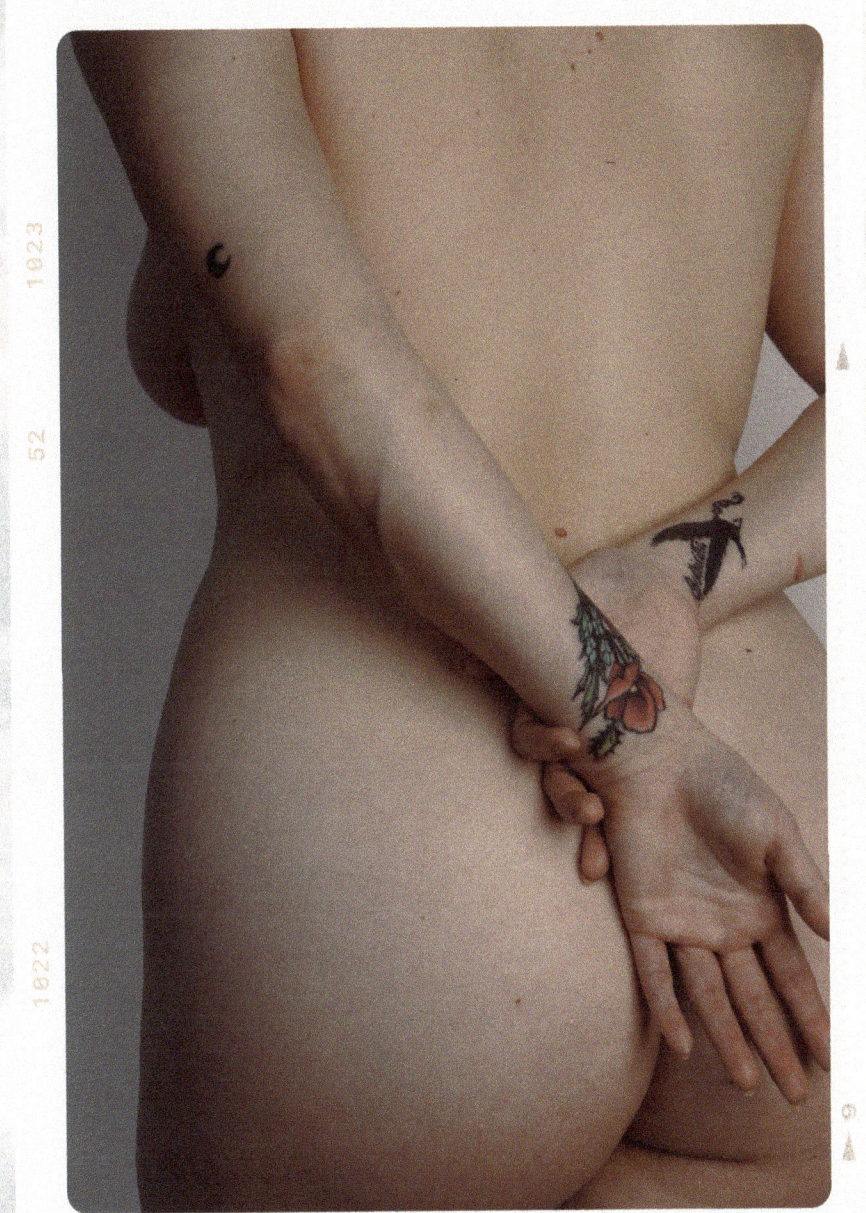

Complacency is the cruelest
curse upon my curiosities
My pen holds no power
My tongue too tied to talk
My dreams turn daft
bringing my mind immediate misfortune

A WOMAN WHO MADE *HERSELF* HER MUSE

He's been the most consistent man in my womanhood
but I've never been able to count on him
He's made the most carnal my passions
while corrupting my peace
He's come and gone as quickly as the shifting seasons
He wants but cannot give
He's stuffed me and then starved me
not knowing when again I'd eat
His tenderness used as torture
for he only half commits

He's loved me, lulled me, lured me and left me
Yet assumes he always warrants space
He blows back in like the breeze of the wind
Stirring my soul and manipulating my mind
I've been his friend, his faithful
his foe and his fool

It's been many years and to each other we've played many parts
The romantics, the real thing, the rowdy and the reckless
Always met with open arms but this time brings me pause

I stand back and feel the sweeps of the curtains
as they close on our last show

A tear trickles down my cheek
both bitter and sweet
This shall be my final bow
with him in hand

KARISSA STRAIN

I wish I had a lions heart
I wish I was more brave
Lately I've been keeping quiet
My heart kept hidden in it's cage

The vulnerability of my soft crab shell
has me retreating to the solace of the cave
The rock walls protect me, the dark soothes my soul
nursing my wounds, fresh from all I gave

I long to live in the light of the day
Clear the clouds, in the sun I'd bathe
Free my heart, lift my soul
creative company is all I crave

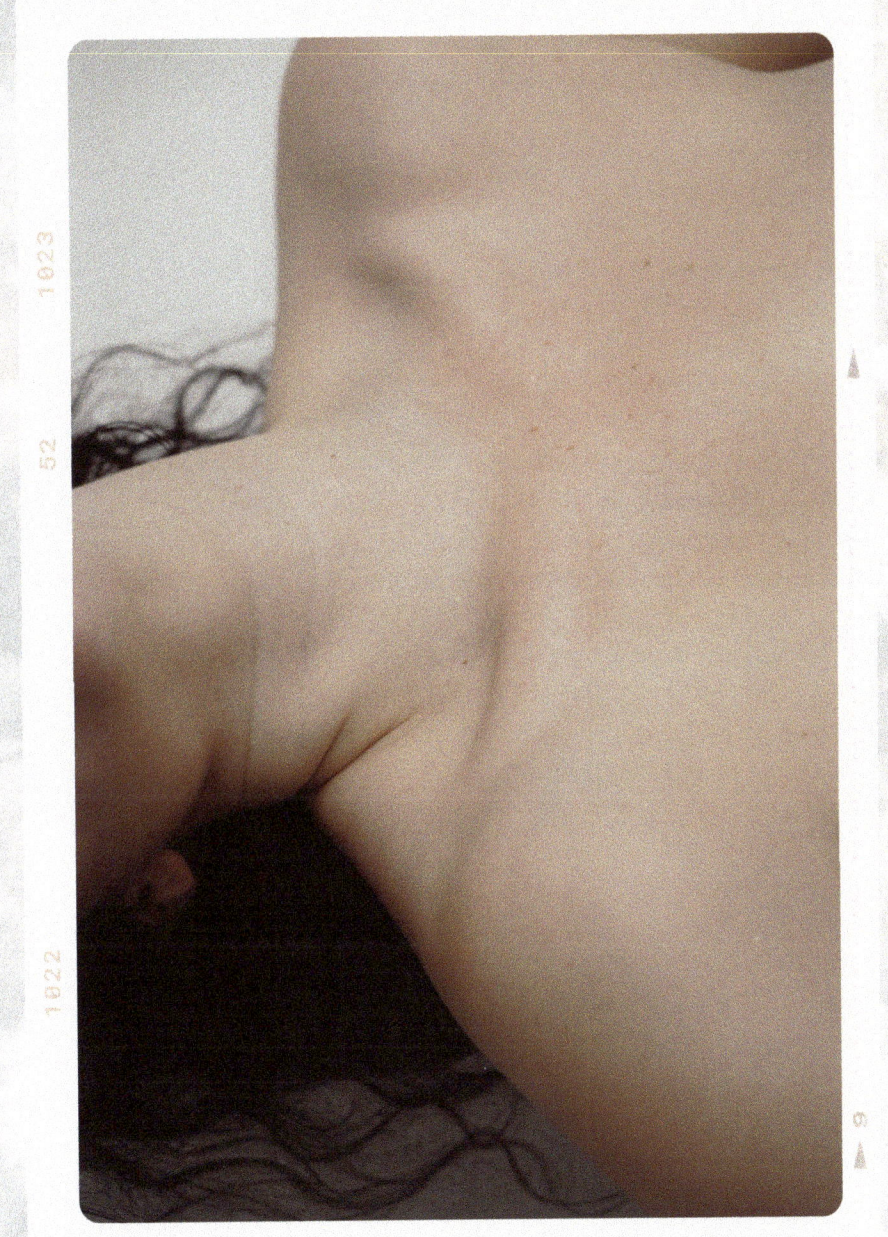

I often think romantic thoughts of times of old
but what if they were never all that romantic?
Most starlet's lived lonely lives of failed marriages
substance abuse
a world that envied
not knowing all they lacked

For a while I've wished our world was still like theirs
Longing to be a film actress
before the days of social media and Tik Tok
changed what it means to "create" art

Perhaps even then I wouldn't have had
the stamina to endure it
The lonely lifestyle of the name in lights
would surely have found my sensitive soul deeply devastated

So much passion dwells within me
Stories and visuals
and I wish for an outlet
but maybe it's time to face the reality

Maybe it's just not meant for me

Maybe I've changed

Things that once seemed important to my ever eager heart
are no longer what keeps my heart beating

The question now is do I give it all up entirely
or is there a way to create in this modern world
that won't take my soul with it?

A WOMAN WHO MADE *HERSELF* HER MUSE

Heavy hangs the hapless air
ripe with rife and expectation
A boiling bellow about to be born

Tricklings of turmoil
toil with the skyline
it can't camouflage behind it's clouds

The humidity slowly edges off
with each breeze softly blowing by
bringing relief to my dampened skin

This chair calmly rocks me
but I'm not fooled by it's tranquility
There shall be no peace in the presence of this night

The leaves have turned their backs to me
and the hostas hang their heads low
They've no wish to face it with me

The inevitable
The unalterable
Mother nature's untimely release

Thunder rolls as the dog whimpers
He mirrors the leaves and the hostas
Ready to head inside and hide

But something keeps me firmly planted

I don't fear it, for I feel it
I know it because it is mine
I too await my release

Will mother nature let me follow her footsteps
I feel the magic in her misery
Maybe I too can make magic out of my own

KARISSA STRAIN

I dream of men succinct and clear
A wonder of waking warning
Should I hold them close and keep them near
or will my heart be drowned in their storms down pouring
To shed the mask and strip the soul
unburdened the honest essence
Too easily I see the good in them
turn a blind eye to dark lurking presence
My unconscious faith is my true North
be it ancestor, angel or guide
No explanation to justify
but it rights my naïve mind

A WOMAN WHO MADE *HERSELF* HER MUSE

We were both too wild minded
to handle the holiness of each other's hearts
A decade of comings and goings
Always ending with us apart

Heavy hangs the daffodils heads
burdened by the crown of last nights blustery snow
Mother nature neither knows
whether spring comes or winter goes
The seasons matching my hesitation
brought forth by the winds of change
Springing forward with hopeful blossoms
yet weary of forgetting the frosty pines of winters strength
Perhaps I shall think more cyclically
What's passed can always again become a futures present

Densely laden upon the Earth
this white blanket warms not the budding blossoms in it's embrace
I realize I too must crawl out from under
the perceived comfort of a seasons close
Recognizing the weighted blanket of the familiar
has become more cold than comfort

What colors I might have to show
whence I step into the warmth that will undoubtedly unfold

The sun struggling to shine
through the flurry filled clouds
urges me to follow suit
and shake loose the last bits of frost
from my grasp

Maybe then I'll find
love can be found amongst the lilacs tenderness
in the touch of tulips petals
and bright bleeding hearts
might mercifully melt my own

A WOMAN WHO MADE *HERSELF* HER MUSE

I'm terrified of my own capacity to dream

That those dreams will be my undoing

That their ultimate unfulfillment
will be the death of me

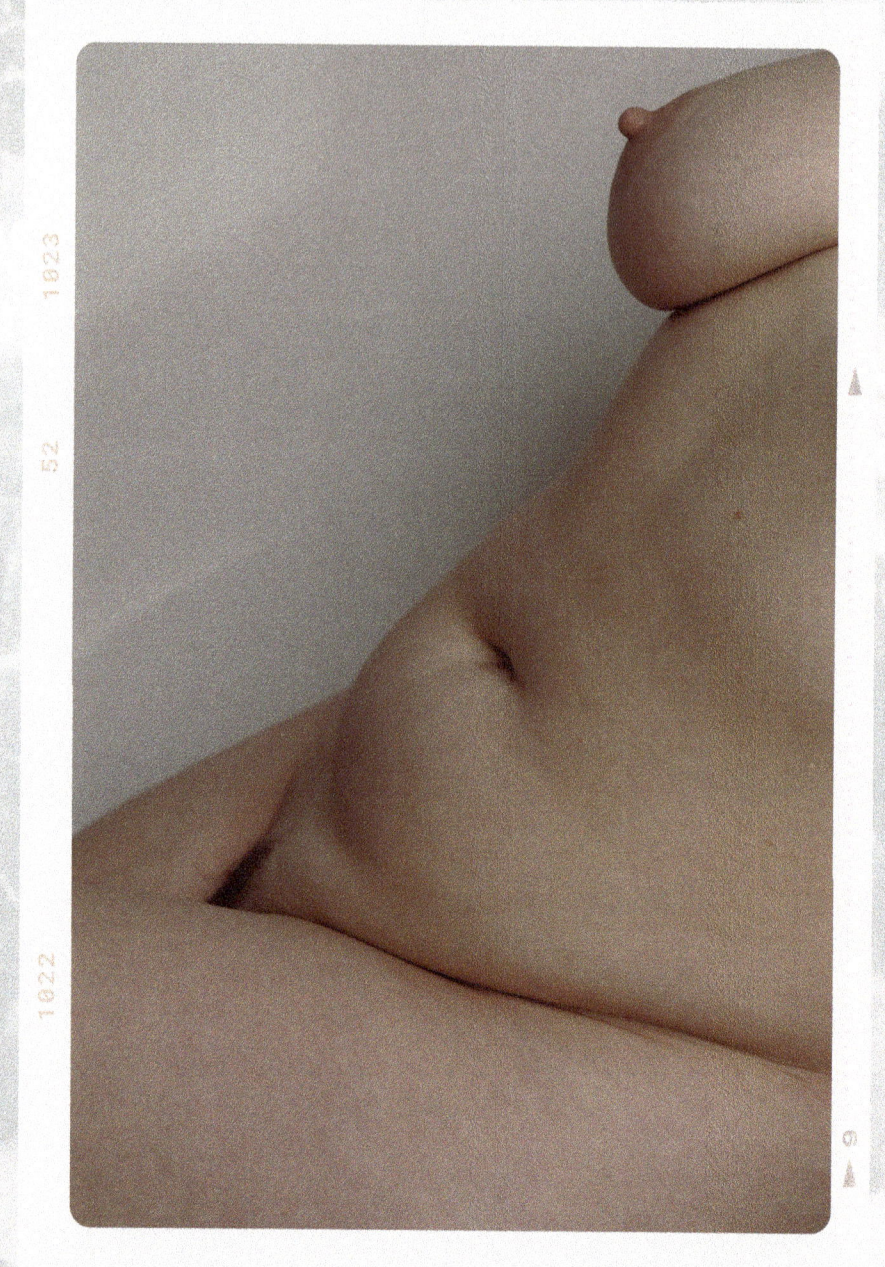

A WOMAN WHO MADE *HERSELF* HER MUSE

Eventually's in the air
I try to grasp like lightening bugs
Should I catch and finally keep them
They'll light the dark in this hole I've dug

If possibility could braid a ladder
I might climb up every wrung
Smell the air and see the sky
Proud of the hook where my hats been hung

Maybes make the best of mountains
For my skylines scenic view
I'd conquer every one of them
From the top sing out my news

If dreams could build a doorstep
Id no longer need to roam
I'd walk right in and stay awhile
Know what it's like to feel at home

He said 'The mockingbird, it mocks me"
It may have been mocking so
but it wasn't him it was mocking
It was mocking the life choices that lead us to be
on this trip in the first place…

It was mocking the dream
It was mocking the move
It was mocking the gamble
The point I'd never prove

It was mocking the desperation
It was mocking the struggle
It was mocking the investment
that I'd far too long juggled

It was mocking the body
It was mocking the drink
It was mocking the dead space
Too much time left to think

A WOMAN WHO MADE *HERSELF* HER MUSE

It was mocking the loneliness
It was mocking the will
It was mocking the return
A hard to swallow pill

It was mocking the passion
It was mocking the desire
It was mocking the purpose
No fuel to feed this fire

It was mocking the madness
It was mocking the muse
It was mocking how easy
it had access to my fuse

It was mocking what I wanted
It was mocking who I should be
No, it was never mocking him
it was always mocking me

The moon could be mistaken for the sun tonight
as it lights up the sky, a candescent sight
I bask in it's warmth
while embraced by the night…

As the nights golden light glows a mark of the harvest
it has me thinking of all I've reaped in the year leading to now
A cornucopia of unknowns, but by far my most fruitful yet
I have aged with the calendar and changed with each season
For the first time in years I feel as free
as the open country roads I walk upon nightly
I breath in the cool air and the familiar scent
of my home town washes over me
It's the ethanol that clouds the clear night sky
as it pours from factory chimney stacks
Mixed with the musky lakes of cleared crop puddles
providing the geese their daily baths
I linger on romantic remembrances of the early evenings
tie dye sky which has seemingly stolen my heart

Why have I never noticed it before now?
I look around
What else have I not noted?

A WOMAN WHO MADE *HERSELF* HER MUSE

I notice towering pines squire my path
A pocket of sky burns red to the North
from greenhouse gasses
There's an army of houses lining my left
like uniformed soldiers
pristine and circumspect
The dried corn hangs low
and flowered wild asparagus grows
along the field ditch
Both past their prime and out of time

Above my head the full moon swells
Crowning the cycle it will restart tomorrow
But tonight I feel no need for ceremony
I no longer wish to leave the luck of my life
up to the magic of the moment

Instead, I shall cling to the tangible sights
and sounds of my surroundings

To the knowing path of the back roads beneath my feet

I trust where they will guide me

At times I feel overwhelmed with the impossibility of life
How big I let my mind wander and how far away it feels to obtain it
I feel sad and sick to my stomach
and I know I shouldn't
I know I should be better
and think brighter
But I feel like a tiny little grain of sand
Inconsequential and constantly trying
Re-thinking
Re-imagining
and scheming different tactics

If I'm supposed to settle for a life of less
If that is my path
My destiny
Then why must I be cursed
with an imagination and a desire
that deeply hungers for more?

My mind is like a beautiful hot air balloon
with limitless heights of possibility
Once it's reached it's capacity
my doubts form rocks
that one by one
weigh the basket of my base
back down to reality

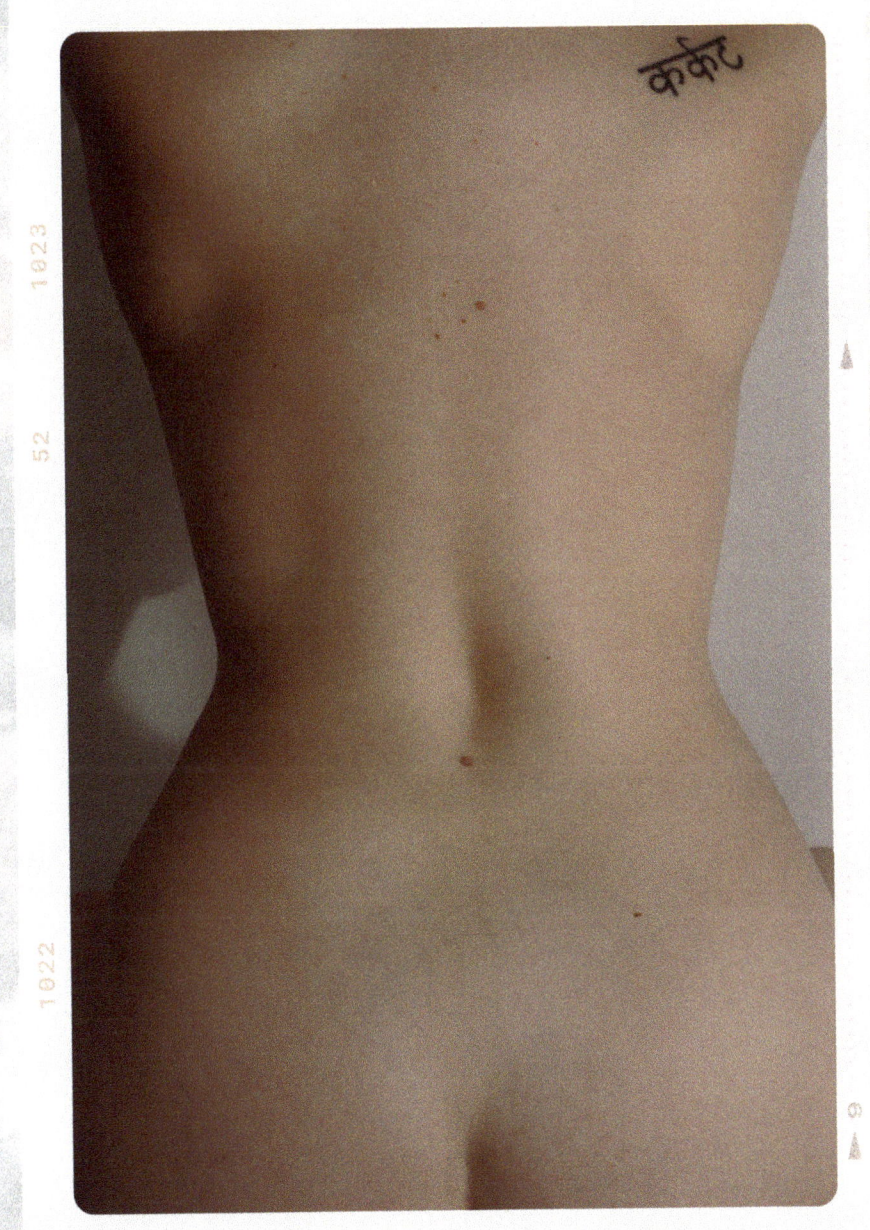

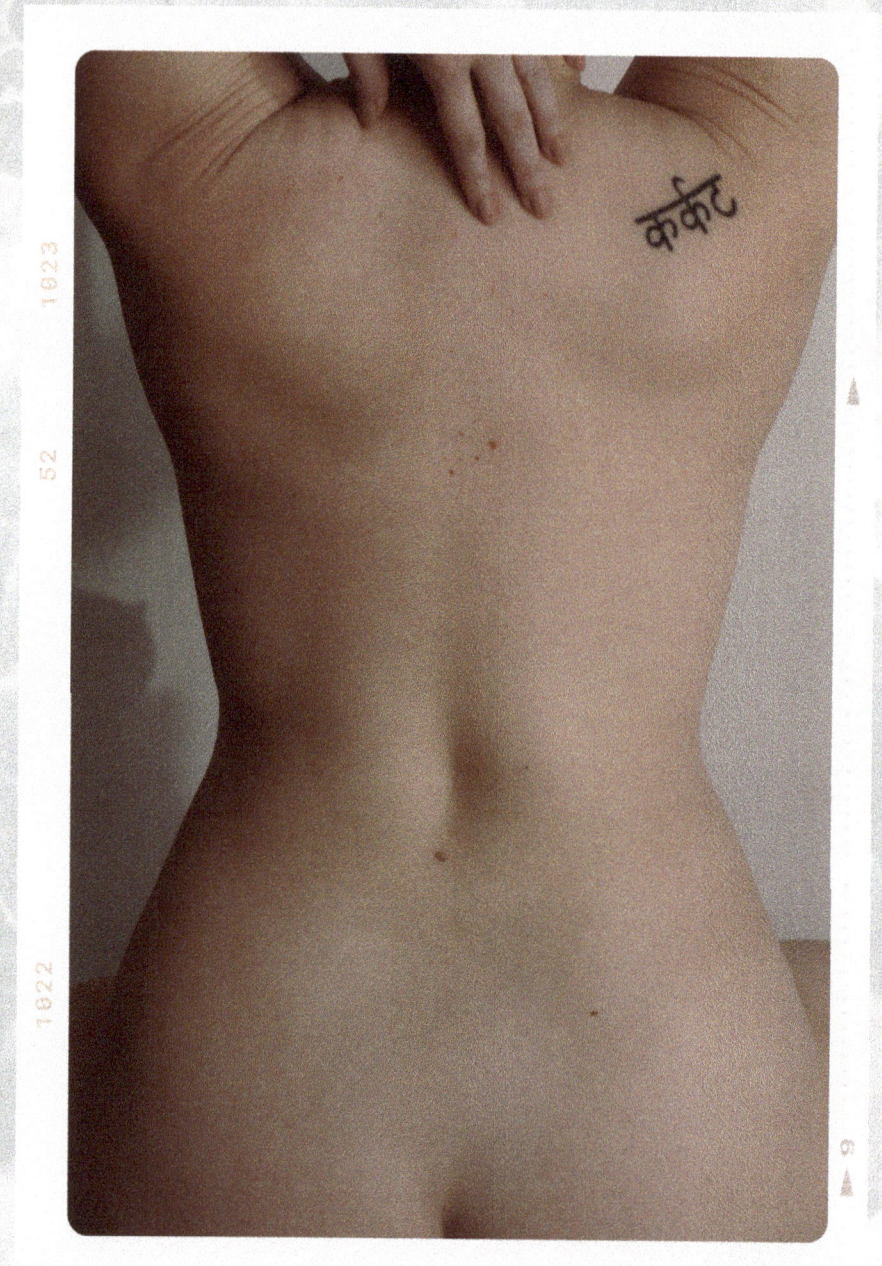

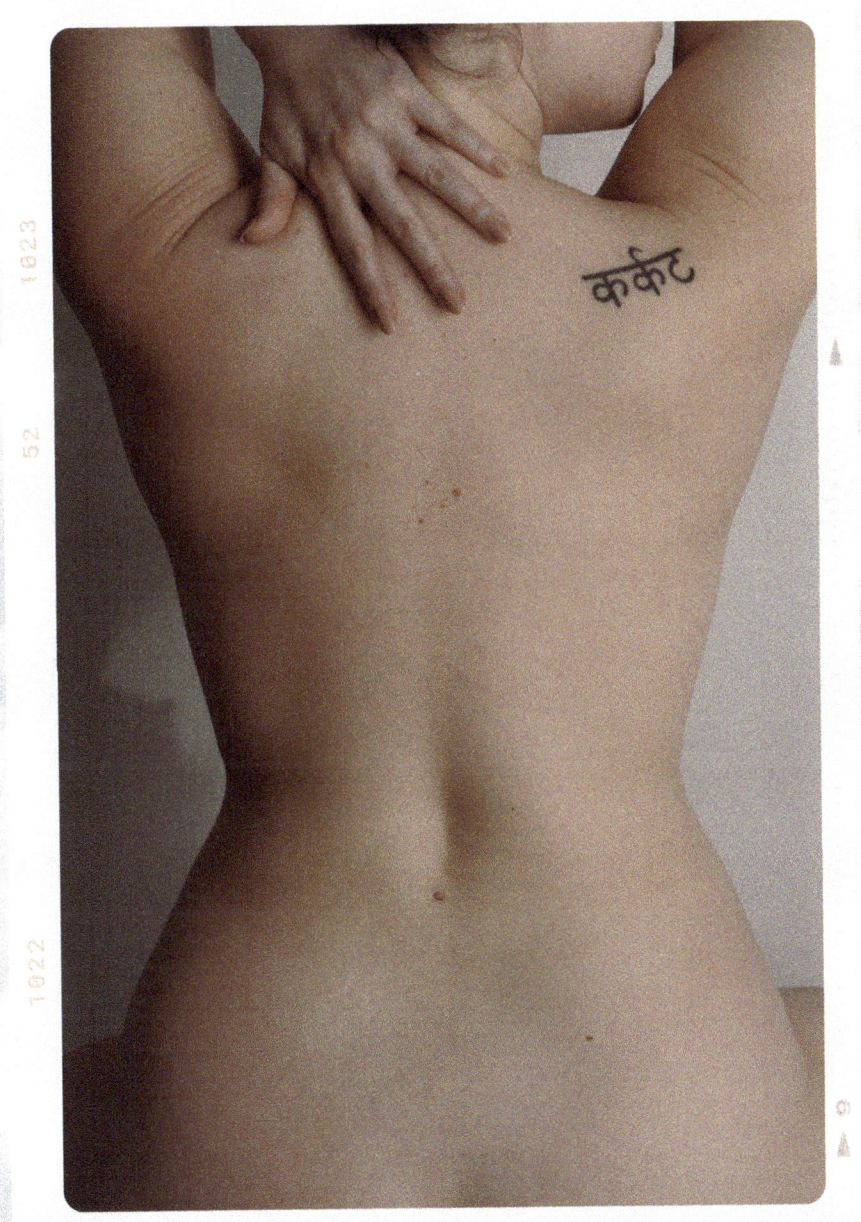

KARISSA STRAIN

I am woman
and I am wild terrain
I am love, I am laughter, I can also bring pain

I am the wolf mother that teaches her cubs a lesson
as she bears and births and then takes them through the seasons
My rivers are wide and they rush but they also give life
My landscape is bountiful and beautiful but can also cause strife

Full of hills and valleys and dips and peaks
For adventure, a journey, the guidance that you seek
My winds will rage and my storms aren't shy
but I give of my fertile soil and I open my skies

I am lush, I am green, I am wise, I am dry
I am soft, I am rough, I am smooth, I am firm
I am warm, I am calm, I am fierce, I am cold
I am everything, I am black, I am white, I am nothing

The absence
The presence
The cause
The effect

Can't live with
and can't live without

A WOMAN WHO MADE *HERSELF* HER MUSE

Yes I am woman
I am wild terrain
My fires burn bright- won't be dampened by my rains
I gather my harvest and share of my gains

I am full, I am complete, I am empty, I am hollow
I'm the muddy soil
I'm the whispering wind
I'm the creaking branches
I am stillness within

I'm the dew that lingers
The frost that scorns
The thunders cry
And the lightening's bolt

I'm the roots that dig deep and thrive in the dark
I'm the branches that reach and yearn for the light
I'm the leaf's unfurling, a sign of great growth
I'm the blossoms brazen pigments, pure beauty they boast

Yes, I am woman
I am wild terrain
I honor the storms
And I weather sunny days

I am bright, I am bold, I am quiet, I am meek
I honor it all, no validation I beseech

Yes- with every breathe, my bounty I own
I am child, I am mother, I am goddess, I am crone

ABOUT THE AUTHOR

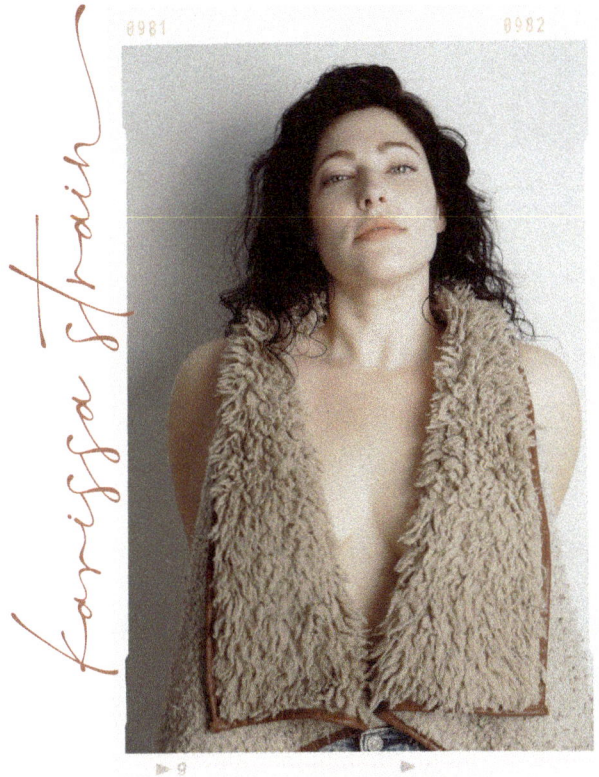

I don't write poetry.
Poetry writes me.
It writes my mood, my actions, my thoughts and my feelings.
It writes my questions, my muses, my curiosities and my disappointments.
It writes my triumphs, my travails, my loves as well as my losses.
For as long as I can remember I have been a very sensitive and emotional person.
I often thought, and through the early years of my adulthood I was often told
(mostly by my romantic partners) that my sensitivities were a shortcoming.
I was too emotional.
I was too soft.
It made me weak, and vulnerable and I needed to work harder to curb
those natural inclinations. I foolishly believed that for a while,
until I learned that my ability to feel deeply and channel those sensitivities
is actually one of my biggest strengths.
My words became my therapy.
My words became my shield from others scorns.
My words became my biggest pride and my constant supporter.
My words became my most fulfilling artistic outlet.
My words became my solace.

For whatever I may lack in life
I will always covet the courage of my words.

www.ingramcontent.com/pod-product-compliance
Lightning Source LLC
Chambersburg PA
CBHW041036020526
44118CB00043BA/3000